How to have a
Big Wedding
on a Small Budget

Cut your wedding costs IN HALF!

FOURTH EDITION

DIANE WARNER

BETTERWAY BOOKS
Cincinnati, Ohio

Disclaimer

Due to the everchanging nature of the wedding industry, neither the author nor the publisher warrant, or are liable for, any information, availability, or reliability of any products, manufacturers, service providers, Web sites or other sources mentioned in this book. Please use your own judgment when dealing with vendors, and access any Web sites at your own risk.

Note: There is no advertising included in this book. Any goods, services, manufacturers or Web sites mentioned throughout the book are included at the discretion of the author; no compensation has been received by either the author or publisher.

Permission

Excerpt from *Diane Warner's Complete Book of Wedding Vows* by Diane Warner. Reprint by permission of Career Press, Inc. All rights reserved.

Library of Congress Cataloging-in-Publication Data

Warner, Diane.
    How to have a big wedding on a small budget / by Diane Warner.—4th ed.
       p.   cm.
    Includes index.
    ISBN 1-55870-646-1 (alk. paper)
    1. Weddings—United States—Planning. 2. Consumer education—United States.
3. Shopping—United States.   I. Title.
HQ745.W37 2002
395.2′2—dc21   2002026191
                                                                      CIP

Edited by Anne Bowling
Production edited by Jolie Lamping Roth
Cover designed by Wendy Dunning
Cover photography by Al Parrish
Interior illustrations by Suzanne Whitaker

To Ron and Lynn
Thank you for letting
me tell your story.
I love you.
Mom

❦

Acknowledgments

I want to thank all of you throughout the country who gave so generously of your time and expertise to help me update this book for its fourth edition, and a special thanks to those wedding professionals and second-time brides and grooms who helped me assemble the new Second Weddings chapter.

Special thanks to all those brides and grooms who shared their ideas with me during my seminars and through their interesting letters.

Finally, my sincere thanks go to my editor, Anne Bowling; production editor, Jolie Lamping Roth; managing editor, Tricia Waddell; and designer, Wendy Dunning, for their conscientious efforts to get this expanded fourth edition to the printer on schedule.

Table of Contents

Introduction: There's Gonna Be a Wedding!

(Getting Over the Initial Shock)

So, there's going to be a wedding! Isn't that wonderful news? No? Maybe not? Of course, everyone is happy that the lovely woman has found the man of her dreams. Are you that woman? Or the mother of the bride? Or, perhaps you're the groom? If the upcoming wedding makes you nervous, the problem is probably money!

If your family finances resemble those of the average American household, you never quite managed to save the money for a wedding. Or, perhaps you're already in debt, and now you discover that you'll need $20,400—the average cost of a wedding in the United States today.

At age twenty-five, our daughter found Mr. Right. He was a fine man, thirty years old, who was also waiting for the right one to come along. They had known each other for two years, both having been active in the Singles' Club at our local church. They had worked on committees together, gone on retreats together and seen each other at least twice a week, but always in large groups. Then, on the last day of May, he asked her out on a real date. At 6:00 P.M. they went to dinner at a little Italian restaurant, and by 10:30 P.M. they were still there, taking turns talking as fast as they could. They realized that they had everything in common—even their interest in astronomy—and before long they were spending evenings in our backyard, studying the stars with our daughter's telescope.

They saw each other every day and it wasn't too much of a surprise when they announced their engagement that August. They wanted to get married at Christmastime! How "storybook" precious! Right? Wrong! I had the same sense of dread you're feeling right now, only I didn't have the benefit of a book like this one to help us plan within our limited budget.

We were living on my husband's income from teaching at a private school, and although I was working, too, my paychecks were being used to help our son through law school. We had decided that when our son graduated we would save all my paychecks toward any eventual weddings. Our daughter hadn't met the right guy yet; surely, we still had time to save. Of course, the timing didn't work out quite that way, but Lynn and Ron had a beautiful wedding anyway—and the price never came close to the national average. In chapter thirteen there's a detailed breakdown of the expenses for our daughter's wedding that will show you how we cut costs, and by following the money-saving ideas in this book, you'll be able to plan a wonderful wedding—even if you have a very small budget.

When we first knew that we would need to plan and pay for a big wedding with only four months' notice, my reaction, after the initial shock, was to go to the city library to search for information. I checked out eleven books, hoping they could give us a grasp of what this wedding would cost. I also asked various people for names of other families who had recently given weddings for their daughters. The library books were very thorough in explaining what is proper and what is not. They told about the hundreds of things to be done and when they should be completed. They told about traditions and trousseaus, gift registries and receiving lines.

Meanwhile, friends related hair-raising stories of a wedding photographer who arrived late, a best man who never arrived at all, a bridal veil that caught fire from a lighted candle, and a groom who fainted as the bride walked down the aisle. All these stories seemed quite amusing to the storytellers, but didn't seem a bit funny to me at the time. In fact, none of the information helped soothe the initial anxiety over the *real* question—how much will it cost?

We had so little time and I felt frustrated. Other inquiries were discouraging at first, too. One of the photographers I called, for example, had prices *starting* at $2,500!

It was through these first fumblings that I discovered that there was not a single book on the market at that time that gave actual costs of a wedding in today's real dollars and cents, much less one that explained ways to stay within a tight budget. That was when I began taking notes for this book, which will spare you, I hope, the frustrations I felt in those first few weeks of uncertainty. In chapter thirteen you'll find several sample budgets within various price ranges, along with four examples of recent weddings in which the brides managed to spend less than $3,800.

This book was not written for the family who can write a check a day between now and the wedding, hire a personal wedding consultant and pay for all the services the consultant recommends. I'm happy for families who can do this; it makes things much easier. The bride (or Mom) doesn't have to act as her own wedding consultant, and she doesn't have to study a book like this one, which was written for families who must squeeze an entire wedding out of the "Food & Miscellaneous" budget. But I'll tell you a secret: If you use the ideas in this book, your guests will assume you did write a check a day, for there are so many money-saving tricks that can be used to create an elaborate-looking wedding.

This book was not written for the family who will be satisfied with an intimate little wedding in the living room with twenty guests and a cookie and punch reception. Or to perpetuate the time-worn joke about holding the cost of the wedding to the price of a ladder—just give it to the groom and let them elope!

This book *is* written for the bride who wants a large traditional or contemporary wedding. She wants to feel very special for this one day in her life, with the walk down the long aisle of a beautifully decorated church or synagogue filled with her family and friends. Or, perhaps she dreams of a fragrant garden wedding or an elegant ceremony on a cliff overlooking the ocean. You *can* plan a wedding like this, no matter how tight your budget, but you'll need to be, among other things, your own wedding coordinator. That means you'll need to have all the facts and you'll need to be very, very organized. This book will give you these facts and help you get organized and stay that way right up to the satisfying moment when you kick off your shoes and smile in relief, knowing it's all over and that it went well.

About This Book

The book you're holding in your hand is the 4th edition, the first having been published in 1990. It has been continually revised and updated through the years and, because it contains more specific wedding costs than other books on the market, it obviously takes a great deal of time and research each time it is revised. As this book goes to print, I found the average cost of a wedding in the U.S. to be approximately $20,400, although costs vary according to the city or state where you live. For example, the New York metropolitan area runs as high as $31,800 and the lower-cost regions run as low as $15,500. To get an idea of where your city or state falls on the cost spectrum, find your state on the table on page 4, and use the table's key to look for your entry below.

High-Cost Regions of the Country

Metropolitan cities in the northeastern states
Metropolitan cities in California
Northeastern states in general
Southwestern states in general

Medium-Cost Regions of the Country

Southeastern states
Northwestern states

Lower-Cost Regions of the Country

Midwestern states
Central mountain states
Rural cities in California

Canadian Prices

In researching Canadian prices, I found them to be highest in the western and central-eastern cities. The Prairie and Atlantic Provinces were the lowest. If you live close to the border, it may be worthwhile to shop for certain items in the United

States. Residents of Vancouver, for example, like to shop in Bellingham, Washington. There you can find turkey for about $1.30 less per pound than in Canada. I spoke with a resident of Florenceville, New Brunswick, who drives seven miles to the nearest American town to purchase her turkey and other dairy and poultry items. I mention turkey in particular because it is a main ingredient of one of my economical reception buffets (explained in chapter six).

Other items you may find at a lower cost in the United States are wedding gowns, shoes and tuxedo rentals. I found the identical tuxedo, for example, renting for $150 in New Brunswick as compared to $85 over the border.

All in all, Canadian weddings and receptions are traditionally longer and more elaborate than those in the U.S., which means you need my cost-cutting ideas more than anyone.

New Wedding Trends

Since the last edition of this book, there have been several new and dramatic changes in wedding trends which we will discuss throughout this book, including:

❦ Bridal gowns are becoming more sophisticated and sexier than ever, many cut on the bias (cut on "the slant" as opposed to "with the grain" of the fabric) for a more sensual, clingy look.

❦ More Thursday-night, Friday-night and Sunday-afternoon weddings, which are less expensive than a Saturday wedding.

❦ Most popular wedding months are June, August and September.

❦ Least popular wedding months are January, February, March, April and November.

❦ More wedding cakes, wedding flowers and reception food are being purchased from supermarkets.

❦ More grooms and groomsmen are purchasing their tuxedos, instead of renting them.

❦ Food stations at receptions are becoming more popular all the time (instead of long buffet tables), with many brides opting for all-dessert receptions that feature a separate food station for each specialty dessert; for example, a "Chocolate Station," a "Sundae and Frozen Yogurt Station," a "Pie Station" and a "Custom Crepe Station." Also, cappuccino and espresso bars are still very popular.

❦ Romantic "flaming" wedding cakes, where every frosted layer of the cake is imbedded with shallow votive candles that are lit when the reception venue is darkened.

❦ More cultural, ethnic and costume-themed weddings, including Halloween Weddings, Renaissance Weddings and Celtic Weddings (see chapter eight).

❦ One-time-use cameras often furnished to the guests during the reception now come in specially designed wedding-themed cases.

❦ More black-and-white wedding photography.

❦ Sharing wedding photos with friends and family over the Internet (see chapter nine).

❦ More couples than ever writing their own vows.

❦ More states are allowing friends and family members to be temporarily ordained to perform the marriage ceremony.

❦ Creating and printing your own wedding invitations on your computer, using innovative new software programs (see chapter ten).

❦ Krispy Kreme doughnuts are the latest gimmicky trend in wedding favors, presenting the wedding guests with fresh doughnuts as they leave the reception. These doughnuts are even being fashioned into wedding cakes (see chapter ten).

❦ More second and third weddings than ever that include children from previous marriages in the ceremony and the personalized vows; the increase in the number of these weddings prompted me to add a new chapter to this edition, written especially for these very special brides and grooms and their children. This chapter also includes sample vows to be used during the ceremonies (see chapter eleven).

In general, couples are becoming more and more creative as they plan their weddings, deviating as far as possible from the cookie-cutter weddings of the past.

By the way, when it comes to selecting your ceremony site and planning the service itself, here are four cost-cutting ceremony trends that are becoming more popular all the time:

❦ Marrying at a simple civil ceremony at the county courthouse with only your attendants as witnesses, followed immediately by a large formal reception. This means you don't have to rent or decorate a sanctuary or formal ceremony site and you won't need to provide transportation for the wedding party from the ceremony to the reception.

❦ Marrying at the reception site itself. Many brides and grooms are choosing to marry indoors in front of their guests (who may be sitting at tables or standing), or on the patio or in the garden of the reception site. This concept worked well, in fact, for our son and his bride when they were married on the flagstone veranda off the reception hall at The Lodge at Pebble Beach in Carmel, California. The veranda was already included in the reception rental fee, so there was no extra cost and it needed no decorations because of the magnificent ocean view.

❦ Marrying at your honeymoon destination. This type of wedding is called a *destination wedding, travel wedding* or *honeymoon wedding* and has become very popular because it saves the cost of a full-blown ceremony and reception. Usually, the couple's closest friends, members of their wedding party and members of their *inner family*, pay their own way to the honeymoon location. Contact the bridal consultant at your honeymoon hotel, or call the visitor's bureau at your honeymoon destination to ask for a list of hotels and resorts that offer this service. It will save you thousands of dollars and, when you return from your honeymoon, if your relatives insist on hosting an informal reception—fine. By the way, some of the more popular destinations for honeymoon weddings are Disneyland in California or Disney World in Florida, cruise ships, and most Las Vegas and Hawaiian resorts.

❦ Marrying at a *surprise ceremony* during a family gathering, such as Thanksgiving, Christmas, New Year's or a family reunion Fourth of July picnic. One couple pulled this off beautifully by having the bride's parents invite an unusually large crowd of friends and relatives for Thanksgiving dinner, including the groom's immediate family members. About an hour before dinner was served the couple's minister arrived to perform the surprise wedding ceremony, followed by the sumptuous Thanksgiving meal which doubled as their wedding feast. After the meal the couple left on a four-day Thanksgiving holiday honeymoon. What an ingenious idea! Their only expenses were the minister's fee and the costs of feeding a larger-than-normal Thanksgiving crowd, and yet they were surrounded by loving (although astounded!) friends and members of their immediate families.

I am happy to be able to share these new trends with you throughout this book, along with updated prices and helpful suggestions gleaned from recent brides and grooms all over the country.

My best wishes go to you—enjoy the book and happy planning!

1

Guess What? You're It!

(How to Be Your Own Wedding Consultant)

"What are you going to be when you grow up?" Were you ever asked this question? Of course you never dreamed you would become a wedding consultant!

A wedding consultant—also known as a wedding supervisor, wedding coordinator or professional bridal consultant—plans, advises, supervises, assembles information, makes decisions, places orders, delegates, organizes, assists, coordinates and generally provides a shoulder to cry on. This unique person provides varying numbers of services and charges a variety of fees.

There are part-time wedding coordinators, often provided by a church, synagogue or wedding venue, for a nominal fee. There are also full-time professionals who may charge by the hour, per service rendered, or up to 15 percent of the total monies expended for the wedding and reception. These amazing people are able to coordinate every wedding service you can imagine. If you decide to hire one of these wedding professionals, you may want to look for one who is a member of a national association that offers special training and requires its members to endorse a strict code of ethics. There are many of these professional organizations, three of which are included in the Resources section (see pages 176-179).

You can serve as your own wedding coordinator, however, and this book will help you along the way. By serving as your own coordinator, you'll not only save money, but you'll provide something even the best trained and most professional consultant never can— LOVE!

Staying Organized Is the Key

There are two things I want you to do before you continue reading this book. The first is to take a deep breath and smile. It will all work out fine. Close your eyes and visualize a perfect wedding. Picture the ceremony, the reception, the happy bride and groom. Envision success with every detail. A positive attitude can make the difference between feeling exhausted or elated after it's all over.

The second thing I want you to do is to purchase a planning workbook or the materials to make one yourself. I have authored a planner specifically designed to be used with this book, which is titled *The Big Wedding on a Small Budget Planner and Organizer*. It's for sale at the same place you purchased this book. Or, you may go to the store with this shopping list:

- A fat three-ring binder

- Loose-leaf paper

- Twelve notebook dividers with tabs and pockets

- Twelve zippered inserts for a three-ring binder

Pick a notebook in a color you love because it will be your constant companion from now until the wedding. This notebook will be used to get organized, and it will be the key to staying calm and within your budget. It will become the indispensable tool in your new role as wedding consultant. Divide this notebook into the following sections:

1. Budget
2. Calendar
3. Ceremony
4. Clothing
5. Flowers
6. Reception
7. Other Food Service
8. Music
9. Decorations
10. Photography and Videography
11. Guest and Gift List
12. Incidentals

In addition to its own divider and plastic zippered insert, each of these sections will also need to be filled with a sizable number of loose-leaf pages, and you'll find it handy to attach a pen to the notebook in some permanent way.

After reading this book you'll have an idea what you should be entering in each of the sections in your notebook. It'll be clear to you as you read along. As an example, the first section of the notebook, "The Budget," cannot be used until you've decided on your wedding budget total, plus allotments for each of the categories within that total.

The Budget

And so, we come to the first section of your notebook. The Budget gets top billing because all your other plans will revolve around the amount of money you have to spend on the wedding. Of course, after reading this book, you'll know how much you can spend on each category and which money-saving tricks you'll decide to use. Chapter thirteen will help you determine the distribution of your total funds into these categories. Then you'll enter these dollar limits boldly and fearlessly, without feeling guilty about the tiny amounts of money you'll be spending. Remember: More is *not* always better and you will have an elaborate-looking wedding without having to auction off the family car. I promise!

The first page of The Budget section will give your overall financial picture, showing the amount of money you can spend for each category, with the grand total shown at the bottom of the page. Following this first page will be one page for each of the eleven categories, with the budgeted dollar limit shown clearly at the top of the page. For example, the page in The Budget section of my notebook marked "Music" showed a dollar limit of $185 and then listed the musicians and what each was to be paid.

After bravely entering your dollar limit at the top of each page in this section, you'll keep track of your *actual* expenses by recording each and every one. Even the cost of this notebook should be noted on the page marked "Incidentals." You'll find that the small costs will add up too fast unless you are careful. That is why many of the money-saving ideas in this book are for the little things. Even borrowing a basket for the flower girl will save the $20 the florist would charge you for it. Eliminating $20 here and $20 there will save you thousands of dollars—you'll see!

Here are the average percentages normally spent on each category of a wedding; they are only guidelines, however, because every wedding is different and the percentages you spend may not resemble these at all:

Reception food and drink	50%
Bride's attire	10%
Photography/videography	10%
Music	10%
Flowers	10%
Invitations and postage	4%
Miscellaneous (decorations, transportation, parking attendants, thank-you notes, garter, ring pillow, guest book, clergyman's fee, etc.)	6%
Total	100%

The Calendar

This section is the wedding consultant's Bible; it's filled with lists of "to dos"—all those things that need to be done at certain intervals before the wedding. For example, since my daughter's wedding was at Christmastime, we had lists of things to be done in September, October, November, the first and second weeks of December and then daily right up to the wedding day. We'll cover the calendar thoroughly in chapter two and I'll frequently remind you to write something down in your notebook, unless, of course, you've purchased *The Big Wedding on a Small Budget Planner and Organizer*, which you'll be using instead.

The Ceremony

Here you'll want to write down the actual order of the wedding ceremony, from the prelude music through the recessional. Fill your zippered insert with a copy of the vows, a copy of the program, a sketch of the layout for the wedding site, whether the site be a church, synagogue, park or private club. You can also use the zippered insert to safeguard the officiant's business card.

Use the pages of this section to write down the names of everyone participating in the ceremony—the bridesmaids, groomsmen, ushers, flower girl, ring bearer, candle-lighters, sound man, ministers, etc. Note their addresses and telephone numbers because you'll need to refer to them often.

Clothing

This will be one of your busiest sections because you, as the consultant, will have so many things to write down and remember. Every item of clothing you or your attendants may possibly purchase needs to be noted, and you should write down the price, and size, as well as the address and telephone number of the store, name of the salesclerk and every other detail you have time to note for each item. You'll find that it's very difficult to remember the exact features of a certain dress or headpiece unless you write them down.

The plastic zippered compartment for this section will be bulging with fabric swatches, ribbon pieces, pictures of wedding and bridesmaids' dresses, price sheets for tuxedo rentals, business cards, brochures, etc. I feel sorry for anyone planning a wedding who doesn't have all this information together in one place. You can't imagine the satisfaction of being able to open your notebook to find a certain name and telephone number, especially when you're in a hurry and don't have time to hunt for it in a drawer somewhere.

When you read chapters three and four on wedding attire, you'll catch on very quickly to the type of information you will need to note in this section of your notebook or the *The Big Wedding on a Small Budget Planner and Organizer.*

Flowers

There are many details you'll need to note in this section because there are so many ways to cut costs here. Keep a very careful record of everything you price, devoting a full sheet to each florist you contact. Place any brochures or written bids into the zippered insert, along with business cards, pieces of floral ribbon and samples of colors. Make note of which florists seem easy to work with, as well as any difference in costs between "in-season" and "out-of-season" flowers.

As you learn about the money-saving ideas explained in chapter five, you'll need to note the comparative costs of using each of them. This will mean recording even the smallest items you'll need to buy or borrow, such as florist wire, baskets, floral tape or plant hangers. This section will be full of prices and ideas that will help you decide upon your floral budget and which plan is the best to stay within it.

If your wedding is scheduled for summertime, or you live in a warm climate, friends and relatives may offer you flowers or greenery from their yards. Be sure to keep a record of each of these possibilities. Write down what type of flower or greenery they have offered and their addresses and telephone numbers for future reference. You may decide to go this "free florist" route and you need to be able to remember who offered what.

The Reception

Here you'll record the costs for all the various food plans. You'll want to write down the exact prices quoted from every caterer you contact and whether these prices are "per person" or "per food item." Then, you'll need to record any cost-cutting alternative plan that interests you, as explained in chapter six.

There are so many ways to save money in this category, without sacrificing an elegant reception, that you'll fill your pages with notes and ideas. When you hear what some caterers charge, you'll love my money-saving tricks. Carefully save all caterers' brochures and price lists, as well as delicatessen prices and grocery costs, in case you decide to purchase the food yourself.

Wedding cake prices fall into this category, too. Make note of prices and save pictures of various styles of cakes in your zippered insert. (Rental of the reception site is covered in chapter ten.)

Other Food Service

"Other Food Service" includes the rehearsal dinner, the bridesmaids' luncheon, pre-wedding snacks for the wedding party and food to have around the house for wedding guests who may be staying overnight. Make lists of what you'll be providing and the costs. Chapter six will help you with these plans.

Music

In this section you'll record the names, addresses and telephone numbers of everyone who will be performing during the ceremony and reception. Write down the fee that each will charge. The zippered insert is wonderful for keeping copies of the music for the ceremony. You can also use this section to record a list of "must play" music selections for the reception.

Decorations

This category includes everything you'll need to give the ceremony and reception sites that certain ambience. This will probably be another fat section, with lots of prices and ideas. I enjoyed planning this part of my daughter's wedding more than any other—it was the most creative and there were so many ways to save money.

You'll also need to write down the names and telephone numbers of everyone who has offered to loan or contribute something toward your decor, whether it be an old-fashioned wrought iron bench to use in the reception hall or pew ribbons you'll be sharing with another wedding at the same site. If you're using my *Planner and Organizer*, this job will be even easier because there are fill-in-the-blank pages to use for this purpose. You'll be saving samples of everything, including ribbon, crepe paper, balloons, napkins and paper plates.

Photography and Videography

This section will also tend to swell with notes. Chapter nine will help you save hundreds of dollars in this category, but, again, you'll need to do a lot of pricing. This will mean a full page for each photographer and videographer, with name, address, telephone number and notes.

When you see various photographers' work, you'll notice that each one has a particular style that will leave you with an impression. Some photographers like to take more close-ups; others prefer outdoor shots. If you plan to hire a professional photographer, be sure to write your impressions of each in your notebook. Do you like the romantic style of one better than another? What do you feel when you look at a certain photographer's work or videographer's video recording? Write these feelings down; they will become invaluable to you later as you make your decision.

The zippered insert, of course, is handy for the photographers' and videographers' brochures, business cards and actual bids. You'll also need to devote several sheets in this section to a list of "must" shots for the photographer. We'll discuss this list in chapter nine.

Guest and Gift List

This is where you'll record the name and address of every person who will receive an invitation. If you ask for an RSVP for the reception, record the response beside each name. In fact, leave four columns to the right of each name and address for:

- ❦ Date Invitation Mailed

- ❦ RSVP Response

- ❦ Description of Gift Received (if any)

- ❦ Date Thank-You Note Mailed

This is a great time-saver when it comes to writing thank-you notes because you'll have the mailing addresses and descriptions of the gifts side by side.

Your sheets could look like this:

Name & Address	Invitation Mailed	RSVP	Gift Description	Thank-You Mailed
Suzanne Smith 125 Main St. Modesto, CA 95380	5/20	Yes	Crystal bowl	8/28
Richard and Susan Wilson Box 395 Cripple Creek, CO 80813	5/20	No	Candlesticks	8/28
Blake Evans 2342 Dawn St. Goshen, CA 93227	5/20	Yes	Place setting	8/28

For your convenience, I've included a blank form on the following page that can be photocopied for your notebook.

In addition to this guest/gift list, this section should have a full sheet devoted to each stationer and printer you contact for prices of invitations or announcements. Also, make note of the particular styles and wordings you prefer.

Your zippered section should contain a copy of the invitation or announcement you finally select.

Incidentals

Here you should include such things as the marriage license, blood tests, hair appointments, postage and other little things that don't seem to fit into any of the main categories. We'll discuss all these pesky details in chapter ten, but this is the section of your notebook for keeping track of them.

Don't forget that the *actual* expenses for all the categories are to be recorded in the first section of your notebook on the appropriate page in your Budget section.

❧

Whether you purchase *The Big Wedding on a Small Budget Planner and Organizer* or create your own notebook, you need to get excited about using it. If you're an organized person, this will be great fun for you. If you're not, try to be organized just this one time in your life. You might like it. You might like it so much, in fact, that you'll

Name & Address	Invitation Mailed	RSVP	Gift Description	Thank-You Mailed

take up a new career after the wedding is over—that of a professional wedding consultant.

The main thing to remember is you must get this notebook set up right away and *use it daily*. It will keep you calm and in control. And, most important, it will *keep you within your budget*. You'll find when it's all over that you had a much more elaborate wedding than you ever thought you could afford.

Acting as your own wedding consultant, you'll feel sorry for those unfortunate people who let the wedding plan them, instead of vice versa. They spend money as they go, getting caught up in the emotion of the moment. They also let themselves be put on a guilt trip. A photographer, for example, may give them a sales pitch that plays on their emotions with the phrase, "This is a once-in-a-lifetime decision . . . you'll be sorry later if you don't buy the more expensive all-inclusive package." Things can easily spiral out of control so that when you get close to the wedding date, you may find you're running out of money. Then, if you're like so many, panic sets in as you frantically borrow against your Visa or MasterCard. Some have even put second mortgages on their homes.

But I know this won't happen to you because, after reading this book, you'll have hundreds of ways to save money and a notebook to keep you on track.

After your wedding is over, by the way, you'll probably find that your notebook will become very popular. Mine did. Many of my friends were planning weddings for their daughters and asked to borrow it. I always said "yes," although my heart was in my mouth—what if they lost it? I not only needed it to write this book, but it has sentimental value to our family. It's full of memories—of the details and the fun we had planning. I shouldn't have worried, however, for my friends always returned it in its original bulging condition, no worse for the wear. And they all saved money by using my ideas.

Don't forget that, as the efficient wedding consultant, you must keep this notebook with you at all times between now and the wedding. You never know when you'll need it because you tend to find bargain items where you least expect them.

My notebook was locked in the trunk of my car whenever I was away from home. Once when I was out shopping for something else I came across a bin of ribbon on sale. Some of the rolls seemed to be the right shade of burgundy, but I wasn't sure, so I ran to the car to grab a color sample out of my notebook. The sale ribbon was perfect and I made the purchase.

I also found treasures at garage sales and, again, it was handy to have the notebook with me. It was at a garage sale, in fact, where I found the burgundy silk flowers I used to make the bridesmaids' headpieces.

The notebook was with me to the end. I almost decided to leave it home on the day of the wedding—after all, the planning was done. But I hauled it with me anyway, and am I glad I did!

Right at the last minute my daughter panicked. It was almost time for her to walk down the aisle and she couldn't remember the wedding vows. She said, "Mom, read me the vows—quick! My mind has gone blank!"

I picked up the notebook, turned to the Ceremony section and took a copy of the vows out of the zippered insert. I read the vows to her, just like the minister would do, and she repeated them to me. This calmed her down and during the ceremony she recited the vows clearly and without hesitation.

My notebook was a good friend and I was so glad I had it with me when Lynn panicked that I even gave it a little hug. Then I looked around, hoping no one had seen me, for surely people would say, "Look, the poor dear has gone bonkers. This wedding sent her right over the edge."

You'll probably hug your notebook from time to time, too, but that will be our little secret—I'll never tell if you don't!

Acting as your own wedding consultant will not only provide you with a creative and satisfying "new career," but will save you a lot of money! As you march off, notebook under your arm, just keep repeating one thing over and over: "I'm saving thousands of dollars . . . I'm saving thousands of dollars. . . . "

So, take a deep breath, picture a perfect wedding, and don't forget to smile. You're in for one of the most creative, satisfying times of your life!

2

Dream It Up
and Write It Down

(Preplanning and the Calendar)

Isn't your notebook beautiful? I'm so proud of you—you're on the path to organization and control! As you noticed, the second section of your notebook is called the "Calendar." This section will contain pages of planning notes, from general to specific. Your preplanning ideas should come first, followed by a very detailed and complete calendar. Think of your preplanning as a broad road and your calendar as little side streets. You must be on the right road or you'll never find the side streets; that's why you need to do some preplanning so that you'll be headed in the right direction.

Preplanning

This stage of your life should be the time when you can sit back in your favorite chair and do a little "right-brain thinking" before we get down to the calendar itself, which by its very nature must be hard and disciplined. We'll get to that taskmaster later in this chapter, but for now, let your mind ponder the big picture. Let it ask questions, such as:

❦ What is my vision of the ideal ceremony?

❦ What kind of theme would be nice for the reception?

❦ What colors do I like?

❦ What month would be best for the wedding?

❦ Do I want to get married out-of-doors?

❦ Who should I invite? What about out-of-town guests?

🐚 How big should the wedding be?

🐚 What role will my future in-laws take in the proceedings?

🐚 Who should I ask to be my maid of honor?

🐚 Will my sister (best friend, cousin) help me with the wedding?

These are some of the things to consider during this preplanning stage. Don't take off running before you're on the right road—that would be a tragic waste of time. Take it slow and enjoy! This may be your only "dreamin' time" between now and the wedding—use it wisely. By the way, dream with the notebook open, for the first pages of the calendar section should be filled with these brainstorming notes.

Visualize Your Ideal Wedding

If money weren't a problem at all, what kind of a wedding would you want? Think back to weddings you've attended. What struck you about them? What stands out in your memory? What touched your heart? Write these things down as you remember them. They may not be as impossible to incorporate into your own wedding as you may think.

How do you want the guests to feel at your wedding? What kind of music do you want played? Can you picture the flowers? What are they? Roses? Close your eyes— can you smell their fragrance right now?

What about your gown? Do you like the drop-waist look? Or do you prefer the fresh and innocent look of puffed sleeves and eyelet lace? Can you picture yourself in one of those sleek, contemporary gowns with the asymmetrical headpiece? Don't be afraid to drool over the expensive designer gowns either, because you may be able to afford a reasonable facsimile if you rent a gown or have a seamstress "knock off" a copy. So, this is the key: don't limit your imagination. By the time you come to chapter three, these dreams may become possible by using one of our magic cost-cutting plans. Look through bridal magazines and see if you begin to sense a mood, a feeling—yes, even a theme for your wedding.

Themes will be covered in chapter eight, but you should be thinking about them now. There are traditional themes, such as Hearts and Flowers, Cupid and Love Doves, or Winter Wonderland. Some of the nontraditional party themes for the reception include Polynesian, the fifties, the Roaring twenties, or a Ship's Cruise. The theme for the ceremony may be fairly traditional, but the trend for the reception has been to toss out the old and bring in the new. Let your mind settle on that thought for a moment and if any ideas come drifting by, grab them and capture them in your notebook; they might come in handy when you come to chapter eight.

One thing you'll find as you read this book is that a wedding is a lot like a play or theatrical production, performed on a beautiful stage. The audience, or wedding guests, don't notice that the "sets" are fabricated, because the overall effect is magnificent. I'll teach you how to work this magic so that your wedding day will seem out of this world. Meanwhile, let your dreams take over, for anything is possible.

Now, close your eyes and listen for a moment. What do you hear? Violins? A harp? The magnificent strains of an organ? A gentle piano? Before everyone begins offering you advice on who should sing at your wedding, or who is a good pianist or flautist, set up some priorities in your own mind. Do you want a quiet, classical kind of wedding and reception with soft piano music? Or, how about the tender sounds of a guitar? These are thoughts to ponder. Don't make a decision today, but become aware of the possibilities. Write down your impressions in your notebook. Be ready for the decisions when they need to be made in chapter seven.

When you walk into the reception on the arm of your new husband, what do you see on the buffet table? Finger sandwiches? French pastries? Jot down the yummy things you envision being served at your reception. Picture the guests as they celebrate with you.

By the way, what colors did you see in the reception? Yes, you'll need to decide on a color scheme that will be carried throughout your wedding and reception. What colors have you seen at recent weddings you've attended? Is there a color that is very special to you? One that makes you feel joyous and uplifted? Jot it down in your notebook and watch for color samples the next time you're out and about.

Where would you like to get married? In a church? Beside a roaring surf? In a rose garden? Don't let anyone pressure you into getting married inside a building if you dream of getting married outdoors. If you want ideas for outdoor sites, by the way, see chapter ten.

Don't let tradition bind you; have your wedding wherever you want. It's your dream.

How about the ceremony itself? Have you always wanted to write your own vows? Ask your clergyman about this idea; it's entirely possible. Many couples are composing their entire ceremonies, as well as their vows.

If you would like to write your own vows, I have written a book that may be helpful entitled *Diane Warner's Complete Book of Wedding Vows* that offers over three hundred vow phrasings, from contemporary to classical.

Picture the wedding party, your handsome groom, his smiling mother. In fact, picture a perfect day in every way—the kind of ideal wedding day you've always dreamed of having. The experts say that you can make things happen by creating a positive image in your mind, so visualize perfection in every detail, and your dreams will come true.

A Little Wedding Etiquette

At an exciting time like this, who wants a lesson in etiquette? I admit this doesn't sound like the most interesting of topics, and I hate to wake you so abruptly from your pleasant dreams, but a certain amount of the preplanning has to do with etiquette.

It's impossible for me to cover everything you need to know on this subject because it would fill an entire book; however, I'll touch on a couple of things that pertain to preplanning, and you can read the rest in a good wedding etiquette book. I recommend *Emily Post's Complete Book of Wedding Etiquette,* by Elizabeth L. Post, available in your local library. It will answer hundreds of questions, such as "Where do I seat the bride's divorced grandparents and their new spouses?" This is a touchy question and obviously needs an answer from Ms. Post.

Meanwhile, your most immediate planning should involve a meeting with your future in-laws. It's a good idea for the bride, groom and both sets of parents to sit down and discuss who will pay for what part of the wedding festivities. The rehearsal dinner, for example, is usually provided by the groom's parents, who may also want to help with some of the reception costs. Of course, in the case where the bride and groom are footing all the bills, it isn't necessary to discuss expenses with the parents, but it's always considered proper etiquette to arrange an introductory meeting between them so they feel included in the plans.

It's also not too soon to discuss hotel or motel accommodations for the days of the rehearsal and wedding; usually the parents of the groom agree to pay for their own accommodations, but the parents of the bride offer to arrange them. Of course, if everyone lives close by, this isn't a problem.

At this time, it's also a good idea to discuss the guest list. The groom and his parents should provide the bride and her family with their list so that the correct number of invitations can be ordered as soon as possible. Invitations should be addressed and ready to mail six to eight weeks before the wedding, and they take about a month to have printed.

Don't be afraid to bring your notebook to this meeting; as all these decisions are made, especially regarding the plans for the rehearsal dinner, make notes in the proper sections of your notebook. Anything regarding the rehearsal dinner should be noted in section seven, and decisions regarding the accommodations should be entered in section twelve.

You aren't the only one who needs to know about wedding etiquette; others in the wedding party are also expected to behave in a certain way. Whether they will or not remains to be seen, but this is what is expected.

Best Man

The best man is an all-purpose kind of guy. He has many responsibilities. In general, he must see that everything runs smoothly. He encourages the groom when he feels stressed; makes all the bride and groom's travel arrangements; supervises the ushers; serves as an official witness to the vows; safeguards the rings and marriage license; pays the clergyman's fee; and proposes a toast at the reception. He also returns all the rented tuxes. His final duty is to be sure the wedding party lines up properly for the "wedding parade" through town, if there is to be one.

Maid or Matron of Honor

She is the person the bride turns to for help. She helps address invitations and records who sends gifts. On the actual wedding day she has many duties: she distributes all corsages and boutonnieres; helps dress the bride and bridesmaids; holds the bride's bouquet and the groom's ring during the ceremony; serves as an official witness to the vows; arranges the bride's train during the ceremony; helps the bride change into her going-away outfit; and collects the bride's attire for safekeeping.

Groomsmen

The groomsmen are very important members of the wedding party, for they make the first impression on the guests as they arrive; they greet the guests and seat them on the proper side of the church. Immediately before the ceremony two of the groomsmen seat the groom's mother and then the bride's mother; after the ceremony they escort them down the aisle. Groomsmen should be available to assist the bride's mother at any time with last-minute details and they should add to the festivity of the reception by introducing guests to each other. The other major duty of the groomsmen is to arrange transportation of the bridesmaids to the wedding site. By the way, although groomsmen usually do double-duty, also serving as ushers before the ceremony begins, in many cases there are two sets of men: groomsmen *and* ushers. In this case, the ushers seat the guests.

Bridesmaids

The bridesmaids should be called upon to help the bride at any time before the wedding. They can help make wedding favors and run errands for the bride or her mother during the last week. They have no official responsibilities on the wedding day other than to look pretty and add to the festive spirit.

The Calendar

This brings us to our lifesaver—the calendar. Don't you feel sorry for those poor people who are trying to plan a wedding without a timetable? You'll learn to depend on your calendar, and it will let you know where you stand at any moment. Set up one page in your calendar section for each month before the wedding. Then set up a separate page for each of the three weeks before the big day. The last few days before the wedding will be filled with intricate details, and you'll need a full page for each one.

It's ideal to have a year to plan a wedding; however, six months can be plenty of time. If you only have three or four months, it can still be done, but you'll feel a little more rushed because you'll be cramming all the "As Soon as Possible" duties into one month's time. Also, you may have to take second or third choice of florist, caterer, minister, musicians and photographer. Your wedding gown may have to be sewn or bought off the rack. Our daughter, for instance, bought her dress one afternoon and walked out of the shop with it in her arms. It happened to fit perfectly and she could have been married in it that evening if necessary.

We planned our daughter's wedding with only four months' notice, and we were very fortunate that we only had to take second choice in one category—the caterer.

But we were very pleased with our second choice, and it probably worked out for the best anyway. When I look back on it now, the main disadvantage of this tight time schedule was the lack of "dreamin' time" as I described earlier in this chapter. We couldn't afford that luxury. As soon as the engagement was announced, my daughter and I hit the ground running and never stopped right up to the wedding day. If we would have even had six months, it would have been a great help. But at least we proved it can be done, and done right, in only four months.

Here are the recommended duties to be entered on your calendar; copy them onto your calendar pages. Then, as each duty is completed, check it off with a big fat felt-tip pen!

Wedding Calendar: What to Do When

As Soon as Possible

- Select the date and time of the wedding. (Be sure to read chapter six before deciding on a time.)

- Reserve the ceremony and reception sites.

- Choose the members of the wedding party.

- Decide on the color scheme and theme (see chapter eight).

- Set a firm budget; enter it in your notebook's Budget section.

- Apply for passports, visas or certified copies of your birth certificates, if needed for your honeymoon travel and marriage license.

- Meet with the parents of the groom.

- Make an appointment with the clergyman or rabbi.

- Start the guest list (make three lists: "must be invited," "should be invited," "would like to invite if possible").

- Begin planning the reception.

- Select the wedding gown.

- Choose mothers' dresses.

- Select the bridesmaids' dresses.

- Arrange for the junior bridesmaids' attire.

Four Months Before the Wedding

 Finalize plans for the reception. Note which things can be assembled ahead of time by friends and family who have volunteered to help.

 Complete guest lists.

 Shop for wedding gifts for each other.

 Order invitations, announcements, thank-you notes and napkins.

 Order the wedding cake.

 Select a photography/videography plan.

 Select a floral plan.

 Select a music plan.

 Select the food plan and begin baking and preparing foods that can be frozen ahead of time, if necessary.

 Decide on your decorations.

 Reserve your wedding night bridal suite.

 Engage volunteers to help with the reception, flowers, photography, music, decorations and any other items. Write down their names and telephone numbers in your notebook. Designate supervisors for each category.

Three Months Before the Wedding

 Plan the ceremony, including the writing of personalized vows, if desired.

 Reserve the rental of the men's wedding attire.

 Schedule a medical appointment for blood tests at least a month before the wedding day.

 Have your teeth cleaned and checked; consider bleaching your teeth with an affordable over-the-counter treatment.

 Begin addressing invitations.

Two Months Before the Wedding

❦ Purchase or borrow the small items, such as the ring pillow, garter, guest book, etc.

❦ Make up the list of "must" photography and videography shots.

❦ Arrange for the rental of certain items that are part of your cost-cutting plans.

❦ Mail the invitations.

❦ Practice hairstyles for your wedding day.

❦ Be sure you'll have something old, new, borrowed and blue for your wedding day (and a sixpence or penny for your shoe).

❦ Begin writing thank-you notes for any shower or engagement gifts received to date.

❦ Select the specific music to be performed during the ceremony and reception.

One Month Before the Wedding

❦ Apply for the marriage license.

❦ Send a wedding announcement to the local newspaper.

❦ Plan the bridesmaids' luncheon.

❦ Schedule final fitting for wedding gown, if necessary.

❦ Wear your wedding shoes around the house, to break them in.

❦ Coordinate the rehearsal dinner.

❦ Start addressing wedding announcements, to be mailed the day after the wedding to those who won't be attending.

❦ Write thank-you notes as gifts arrive.

❦ Borrow luggage for your honeymoon, if necessary.

❦ Have final meetings with the florist, caterer, photographer and musicians, or the volunteers helping on one of the cost-cutting plans.

❦ Arrange accommodations for out-of-town guests.

Three Weeks Before the Wedding

❦ Arrange for all the men renting tuxedos to be measured at the rental shop.

❦ Finalize rehearsal details.

❦ Arrange transportation for the wedding party to and from the ceremony site and the reception site.

Two Weeks Before the Wedding

❦ Confirm the reception guest list and inform the caterer of the number.

❦ Pack for the honeymoon.

❦ Deliver list of "must" shots to the photographer and videographer.

❦ Hire nursery workers to care for small children, if necessary.

❦ Sit down with your family and your fiancé's family to determine ceremony seating for family members and special guests; give the list to the ushers (or Best Man) during the wedding rehearsal.

❦ Make out a seating plan and prepare place cards for the rehearsal dinner.

❦ Arrange for the transport of your gifts to your home on the wedding day.

One Week Before the Wedding

❦ Make up and mail, fax or e-mail a time schedule to everyone involved in the wedding.

❦ Confirm one last time with the florist, caterer, photographer, etc.

❦ Confirm honeymoon reservations, bridal suite reservations for your wedding night, pick up airline tickets and purchase travelers checks, if necessary.

❦ Have final, final fitting of the wedding gown.

❦ Attend the bridesmaids' luncheon.

❦ Confirm rehearsal plans with the officiant.

❦ Pack boxes of supplies for the rehearsal, wedding and reception.

Daily During the Week Before the Wedding

You'll have daily lists of things to do that are unique to your own wedding. My family teased me because of my detailed lists. Whatever I didn't get done one day, I transferred to the next until there was no time left. The only major thing we forgot was the marriage license. It should have been given to the minister ahead of time, but a half hour before the wedding was to begin, the minister came to me and asked for it. I said that I didn't know where it was—I thought the groom was responsible for it. Well, it turned out that the groom had given it to our daughter, who put it on her dresser for safekeeping. The minister refused to marry them without it. So my husband drove home, found it among her things and returned just in the nick of time. Everything came off on schedule, and no one ever knew of the temporary crisis. The lesson to be learned from this is that, as wedding coordinator, you need to follow up on everything. Don't assume anyone will remember anything, even if it does make you feel like a drill sergeant at times.

There is one very important thing for you to remember: You won't have to do it all alone—learn to delegate! You'll have dozens of friends and relatives who'll ask if there is anything they can do to help. After reading this book, you'll not only have cost-cutting plans for staying on your budget, but a nice fat list of things for your volunteers to do as well.

If your ''wedding consultant hat'' is feeling awfully tight about now, take it off for a moment and relax. I wore that same hat, so I know the overwhelming responsibility you feel but, trust me, the fears will ease as you get used to your new role. Your anxieties will be replaced by warm feelings of satisfaction as you see the results of your planning.

❦   ❦   ❦

3
She'll Wear Satins and Laces...
(Become a Cinderella Without a Fairy Godmother)

You have your notebook open and ready and your calendar is by your side. All you need is something to coordinate. How about the purchase of the wedding gown? After all, the wedding is six months away, and it's time to make this important decision! You'll find as you do your planning that nothing compares with the excitement of selecting the bride's attire. When other subjects are discussed, such as the photography, flowers or filling the guests' tummies with food, the bride will smile politely and offer her suggestions. But when we talk about her gown, she sits up straight, her eyes sparkle and her attention span increases dramatically.

The wedding guests are interested in her gown, too. You rarely hear a guest asking, "What are they serving at the reception?" or "What kind of flowers did they choose for the chapel?" The questions most often asked before the wedding are: "Have you seen her wedding gown?" "How long is the train?" "What does it look like?" "Has the groom seen it yet?"

On her wedding day the bride becomes the center of attention, and that's why her gown is the most important purchase. But, it doesn't need to be an expensive one to be memorable.

In this chapter I'll give you some good ways to cut your costs on all the bridal accoutrements, and you can do so without sacrificing style or quality. You're probably worried that I plan to drape the bride with lace tablecloths, or something equally tacky, but dismiss such horrible thoughts from your mind! I promise she'll make a breathtaking picture as she glides down the aisle in her exquisite gown.

My daughter and I didn't go about it in the smartest way. We bought her wedding gown at a full-price, retail bridal salon! This is obviously the most expensive way to go but, unfortunately, I didn't have a book like this one to explain the cost-cutting alternatives.

When our daughter became engaged, her first reaction was to try on wedding gowns. We bought bridal magazines and drooled over the gorgeous styles. There were stacks of these magazines on our coffee table with dog-eared pages marking her favorite dresses. It was such fun to ponder the choices, while leisurely nursing a hot cup of coffee. This was followed by many trips to bridal salons where she tried on six or eight dresses each time. Some styles were more flattering than others, and we made note of the particular gowns that were possibilities.

We also hounded the bridal salons in the finer department stores. It took a month of looking before our daughter found the perfect gown. It happened quite unexpectedly, in fact. One day we asked my mother-in-law to go gown shopping with us. We thought this would be fun for her, and since she was in poor health, we selected a small bridal salon close to her home. We didn't expect to find the right wedding gown in such a small shop, but since we were going there for Grandma's benefit, it didn't really matter. Of course, that is the very shop that had the perfect gown. We bought the dress right off the rack, plus the headpiece and veil, and slip, and later purchased some satin slippers. Her gown cost the equivalent of about $1,200 in today's prices, which is about the average cost of a wedding gown in the United States as this book goes to print.

Although we had a very positive experience with the sales staff at the little bridal shop where we bought her gown, I've come to realize through years of research that there are certain precautions that should be taken when dealing with a private retail salon. First, be aware that in some cases the sales staff may be on commission, which may cause the salesperson to praise every dress you try on.

Another problem with a few of these shops around the country is that they ask for your name, address, telephone number, time and place of the wedding, and some may use this information for profit by *selling* it to florists, caterers, photographers and consultants. These pushy people will call you, usually during the dinner hour, not only robbing you of precious time, but exerting sales pressure. It's a lot like inviting a vacuum cleaner salesman into your living room—not much fun!

Another complaint I've heard is that a few bridal salons may encourage the bride, and other members of the bridal party, to order larger sizes than they need because they want to be able to charge you later for an alteration fee. Several bridal salons I checked have bridal alterations *starting* at $250! So, beware of this ploy! Ask to see the manufacturer's sizing chart and use your own judgment when ordering a bridal gown.

In fairness to the thousands of honest, ethical bridal salon owners throughout the country, I will say that, fortunately, not all salespeople fall into this category and, in fact, a bridal salon may work well for you, especially if you find a gown you like that fits you right off the rack, or if you happen onto one of their marvelous sample sales. Fortunately, my daughter's size 12 wedding gown fit her perfectly and we took it with us that very day.

In addition to the cost of the wedding gown, you'll also need the headpiece and veil, shoes and petticoat. The headpieces and veils start at about $125, the shoes around $90 and petticoats $100.

Now that we've thoroughly depressed ourselves with these figures, let's move on to the good news! I have eight cost-cutting ideas for you.

Prices in each plan are for the wedding gown only; cost-cutting ideas for the headpiece, veil, petticoat and shoes are given later in this chapter.

The Bride's Dress

Something Borrowed
Approximate Cost *$75*
___

The total cost for this plan is the price of an alteration, if it's required. The gown may be one you've borrowed from a friend, or it may be a family heirloom.

If you borrow a gown from a friend, be sure she has been married for at least a year. She deserves to feel like Cinderella for the first year and really shouldn't loan out her dress. After a year, of course, she feels like an "old married lady" and is glad to share her gown with a friend. It's very important, by the way, to have the gown altered back to its original size after you've worn it. This can be done by recording the exact measurement a seam is taken in or let out. A large stitch (size 7) is preferable to avoid seam marks.

In the case of an older wedding dress that belongs to the bride's mother, grandmother or other relative, it will probably need to be mended or dry-cleaned before it can be worn.

In any case, if you borrow your wedding gown, be sure to have it dry-cleaned before returning it.

Rent It
Approximate Cost . . . . *$150 and up*
___

If I knew then what I know now, this is the idea I would encourage. When our daughter planned her wedding, I didn't know you could rent wedding dresses. Since that time, however, I have seen so many breathtakingly expensive dresses that have been rented, I feel this is a realistic choice. By the way, these gowns can usually be altered.

You can spend up to $500, or more, if you want to rent a more expensive gown. A rental company in Seattle, for example, advertises that their $350 rental dress "retails for $1,500." It's not necessary to go this high, however, as the lower-priced rentals are for wedding gowns that would normally retail from $900 to $1,200.

Rental prices vary from shop to shop throughout the country. The main problem you'll have is finding a good shop close enough to your hometown. All the larger cities seem to have wedding attire for rent, and many of the smaller cities do, too, but you may have to drive thirty or forty minutes to find what you want. These rental stores can be found in the yellow pages under:

❦ Bridal Attire

❦ Costumes

❦ Wedding Rentals

❦ Rentals

Note: Look for a Formals, Etc. or An Alternative (see Resources on pages 176-179).

"Prom It"
Approximate Cost *$140*

Have you noticed prom and special occasion dresses lately? Many can easily be converted to a wedding gown. If it's a strapless gown, you can add detached puffed sleeves, a lace jacket or a train made out of the same type fabric or lace. The train can be attached to the top of the bodice or at the waist. Make it detachable so it can be removed during the reception. The bridal party catalog of JCPenney's offers many affordable special occasion gowns suitable for the bride, including a white or ivory sleeveless Scott McClintock gown with a train for only $179. I've also just discovered a marvelous Web site you may want to take a look at: www.bestpromdresses.com. Many of their prom gowns can be easily converted to a wedding gown, as is, or by adding a tulle train or sewing on sequins or tiny pearl beads. One of my favorites is priced at only $125.

When you're shopping for matching fabric, be sure you have the gown with you. If you doubt your own talents as a seamstress, you may want to have this done by a professional.

You should also look in the "after-five" or evening wear sections of your local department store. There are some very sleek and contemporary dresses available here that can be embellished with a train for a sophisticated look.

For example, a recent twenty-seven-year-old bride in Chicago found her wedding dress on the sale rack at Lord & Taylor: an $80 white lace cocktail dress that she remodeled only slightly by removing what she called a "really ugly rhinestone pin" and a "fake chiffon overskirt," resulting in a sleek, sleeveless lace sheath.

Some cities have factory outlet stores; try them for prom dresses or evening wear that can be converted to wedding gowns. San Francisco, for example, is loaded with these stores and is known especially for its Gunne Sax outlet. Outlet stores offer prices up to 80 percent off regular retail, especially JCPenney outlet stores, if you happen to have one near you. See the Resources section on pages 176-179 for more outlet possibilities.

Another source of suitable dresses is the antique store. Very often you'll find an old-fashioned Victorian-style dress for sale alongside an antique chest or brass bed. And don't rule out flea markets, Goodwill or thrift shops, as unlikely as they may seem. I have often found wedding gowns and white evening dresses for sale at such places; they are even wrapped in their original plastic, having been worn only once.

The main thing is to keep an open mind. By embellishing an existing dress, you can have an exquisite, original creation.

Bridesmaid's Gown in White
Approximate Cost $150

Something the bridal shop staff may not tell you is that many brides purchase their dresses off the bridesmaids' rack. Bridesmaids' dresses are often available in white or ivory and are considerably less expensive than the bridal gown. Some of these dresses even have a short train, but if you want a longer one, just add it yourself.

The Distress Sale Dress
Approximate Cost $150

This is a sad thought, but sometimes a wedding gown is bought, but never worn. Maybe the bride found out that her prince was right out of the Arabian Nights—you know, the one with a harem. Or, perhaps, his "rewarding career in the aluminum business" turned out to be collecting empty pop cans from trash bins. In any case, her loss might be your gain.

Here are some recent ads from the classified section of local newspapers:

"Wedding dress, never worn, size 14, originally $950, sacrifice at $100"

"Wedding gown, special order designer gown, size 10, originally $1,200, asking $350"

"Wedding dress, new, $150"

Take a look at some of these gowns; try them on. If the gown seems right, make an offer. In fact, make a low offer. Usually, the owner is delighted to get rid of it. Whatever you do, don't shun a gown that's a size or two larger than you normally wear because you can always have it altered to fit.

By the way, for the "mother of all distress sales," check out eBay (see Resources on pages 176-179). They seem to have a running inventory of a couple hundred gowns at all times.

Free Seamstress
Approximate Cost $190

If you're handy, why not purchase the pattern and fabric and sew the dress yourself? Or you may have a talented aunt or grandmother who would be honored to sew the gown for you. There are many advantages to making your own gown:

- 🐦 You can try on wedding dresses in salons to find a style that is becoming, then buy a similar pattern.

- 🐦 The dress will fit you perfectly.

- 🐦 You know the dress will be ready for the wedding.

- 🐦 It will cost you a fraction of the price of a store-bought gown.

More brides would make their own wedding dresses if they only realized one thing: There is no need to worry about ruining the fabric! Do what the professional seamstress does: make it first out of an old sheet. You don't need to make the entire gown, only the bodice and sleeves. And this preliminary sewing job doesn't have to be neat and tidy either. It just has to give you an idea of the style and fit. If the bride doesn't like her "sheet version," ditch the pattern and buy another one. There are dozens to choose from.

Considering the money that will be saved by making your own gown, what is a little money spent on a few patterns? Try them out, just like you would try on a finished gown. Then, when you have a bodice that fits and flatters, lay the pattern out on the fabric and cut away. The fear is gone—you know the gown will turn out right.

Here are the costs to sew a typical pattern. The price of the pattern is about $15 and it includes two versions of a wedding gown and a coordinating bridesmaid's gown. The wedding gown has long sleeves and an average-length train.

MATERIALS	COST
Pattern	$ 15.00
Fabric, 9¾ yards of 45″ taffeta @ $3.99 per yard	38.90
Lining, 9 yards of 45″ acetate @ $4.99 per yard	44.91
Lace for overbodice and sleeves, 1¾ yards, 45″ @ $7.99 per yard	13.98
Tulle for overbodice and sleeves, 1½ yards, 54″ @ $2.98 per yard	4.47
Alençon Galloon lace, 6¾ yards at 4¾″ wide @ $5.99 per yard	40.43
Thread	1.99
Two ⅜″ buttons for sleeves @ $1.00 each	2.00
One package soutache braid for button loops	2.50

Zipper, 18″	2.60
800 sequins in one package	1.00
200 small pearls in one package	3.25
Fabric glue, one bottle	2.50
Twenty satin-covered buttons @ $.80 each	16.00
Total	$189.53

The prices of these materials are straight out of a local fabric store in the city where I live. None of the fabrics were on sale. If you have the time to shop for bargains, or if you're willing to make the gown from less expensive fabrics, the total cost can be cut by at least another 25 percent. I took these prices just as I found them so you'll know how easy it is to walk into any fabric store and buy what you need.

The mysterious-sounding items called for on the pattern, such as the Alençon Galloon lace or the soutache braid looping, are available in any fabric store. Just ask the sales staff for help—they know where everything is located.

The pearls and sequins, also listed on the pattern, can be glued onto the dress. They go on easily with fabric glue or a hot-glue gun. The pearls, sequins and glue are found in the craft section of the store.

Just remember that you should not purchase any fabric until you've made the pattern up in sheeting first. When you're sure you'll like the gown, go back to the fabric store to purchase your materials.

Hire a Seamstress
Approximate Cost *$415*

Take the same gown described under the "Free Seamstress" plan and hire a seamstress to sew it for you. I had wedding gowns priced out for me by various seamstresses, and their labor averaged approximately $225. A sheath-style, sleeveless gown, with no sleeves and no embellishments would run about $125, an average gown about $225 and a more complex pattern, with overskirt, sleeves and detailed sequin and bead work runs much more, up to $350, just for the labor. But, for an average gown, the materials and labor together would total under $415.

Many of the seamstresses I spoke with will help the bride shop for the pattern and fabric. They'll also come to the wedding with their portable sewing kits in hand to do any last-minute alterations. Some will even shorten or lengthen sleeves on the men's tuxes, replace a button or shorten a hem at the last minute. Most do not charge for this service if they've been hired to sew the clothes for the entire wedding party.

By the way, the one fabric they all seem to advise against is genuine silk. They say it's too difficult to work with, even for the professionals. There are many synthetic "silks" that are just as lovely as the real thing.

These are some of the advantages of this "Hire a Seamstress" plan:

❧ The dress will be well made and will fit exactly right.

❧ There will be much less stress on the bride and her mother.

❧ It may prevent friction within the family just in case a well-meaning relative does a poor job.

Tip It seems to me that, unless you prefer to have the gown sewn for you because you're hard to fit, or you have a certain style in mind that you can't find anywhere else, with the increase in the costs to have a gown sewn since my last revision, you might be better off purchasing a ready-made gown from another source, such as the discount market. Or, you can always purchase a plain, affordable wedding gown (or bridesmaid's gown in white or ivory) and have a professional seamstress add the embellishments.

Buy From a Resale Shop
Approximate Cost . . . . .50%–75% off Retail

Resale and consignment shops have always done a big business in this country. Some of these shops sell all kinds of clothes, some only women's clothes, and some specialize in wedding attire. The larger the city, the better your chances of finding what you're looking for; in fact, many of the big city resale shops carry as many as two hundred resale gowns at any given time. If you live in a small town with limited availability, it may be worth a few hours' drive to your nearest metropolis for the sake of saving hundreds of dollars. Check out the yellow pages and give these stores a chance; you may find just the perfect gown without a four to six month ordering delay and you can take the gown home with you the same day.

Buy Discount
Approximate Cost . . . . $150–$600

The discount market is everywhere, including factory outlets, through catalogs, Web sites and local bridal shows. The Gunne Sax factory outlet in San Francisco, for example, has a separate building just for the sale of wedding attire.

You might check to see if there is a David's Bridal near you (see Resources on pages 176-179); they are worth the trip with average prices running around $500, or less. In fact, as this book goes to press, David's Bridal is running TV ads in my hometown for gowns priced at $99. Also, if you're near Brooklyn, New York, visit Kleinfeld's on 82nd Street; if you live in the Boston area, take a look at Filene's Basement sales (see Resources on pages 176-179); or if you live near either border, price out gowns in Canada or Mexico. Depending on the exchange rate, you may be able to save 40 percent or so in Canada.

Local bridal shows are possibilities, as well, usually held in larger cities around the country. Most of these shows take place on Saturdays, so even if you live a couple hours away, it may be worth the drive.

Another source of discounted bridal gowns is the bridal salon itself; they often offer their "sample" gowns on a special rack, discounted from 25 to 50 percent.

Another way to buy discount is through a discount broker. Yes, there are discount brokers who specialize in bridal attire. One of the best is Discount Bridal Service who has over a hundred representatives throughout the country. They can offer you name brand gowns at 20 to 40 percent off the retail prices. Here is DBS's toll-free number: (800) 874-8794. They'll put you in touch with their representative in your area.

Finally, the current JCPenney bridal party catalog has Sweetheart wedding gowns in the $300 range. (Their bridal party catalog gowns can be special ordered through their Special Occasion Dress departments.) If you're turned off by the idea of buying a wedding gown from JCPenney, you probably haven't taken a good look at what they have to offer, especially at their outlet stores (see Resources: "Wedding Gowns $800 and Under" on pages 176-179).

By the way, wherever you shop, here are my favorite manufacturers of affordable wedding gowns, all of which offer gowns for less than $800 retail, which means that with a discount, of course, your cost will be even less:

❧ Alfred Angelo

❧ Bonny Gowns

❧ Bridal Originals

❧ Forever Yours International

❧ Jacquelin Bridals

❧ Jessica McClintock

❧ Mary's Bridal

❧ Mon Chéri Bridals

❧ Mori Lee

❧ Private Label by G

❧ Sweetheart Gowns

The Bridal Suit
Approximate Cost $160

It has become very fashionable the past couple of years for the bride to wear a white or ivory suit. This idea will save you hundreds of dollars; you can find one in the "After-Five" or "Finer Dress" sections of your favorite department store. The bridal party catalog at JCPenney's is also a good place to look for a bridal suit; their current catalog features an elegant floor length suit, with lace and pearls, for only $169.

The Bride's Headpiece

If you decide to purchase the headpiece and veil from a bridal salon, you'll probably pay between $100 and $350. There's a terrific markup on these items. But, like the wedding gown, there are several ways to save money.

Just remember that whether you buy or make the headpiece, it should coordinate with the dress. Also, the length of the veil depends on the formality of the dress and the wedding itself. If the dress is street-length, the veil should be shorter. If the dress is floor-length and the wedding is formal, the veil should be fingertip length. For a more informal wedding, the bride may wish to dispense with a veil altogether and wear only a hat or flower in her hair.

Also, be sure the headpiece and veil are compatible with the gown. Don't match up an exotic space-age headpiece with a ruffly "Southern belle" gown. If the veil has lace, be sure it's the same style as the wedding gown. Use bridal magazines as guides; they do a beautiful job of coordinating veils with gowns.

Something Borrowed
No Cost $0

Wear your friend's or relative's headpiece and veil. It's become very popular lately, in fact, for the bride to wear her mother's or grandmother's veil, and it can serve as the "something borrowed" for the bride.

Rent It
Approximate Cost $20

You'll find a lovely selection at the rental shops. Again, it's a matter of finding a rental shop convenient to your hometown.

Distress Sale
Approximate Cost $20

Very often the bride who's selling her wedding gown through a classified ad also has her veil for sale. Be sure to ask when you call on the ads because the veil may not be

Styles of Wedding Veils

❦ *Beaded cap headpiece with veil*

❦ *Crown headpiece with flowers and long veil*

❦ *Jeweled headpiece with veil*

Bridal veils are based on either a cap or a headband design. Although they look exquisite, they are so simple anyone can make them—even someone who doesn't sew at all. Fabric stores sell a variety of caps and headbands already embellished with pearls, flowers and lace, or you can put together your own creation. Then simply attach the netting and you'll have a stunning veil for a fraction of the retail price.

advertised as a separate item. You may, in fact, get the veil thrown in for free with the cost of the gown.

Free Seamstress
Approximate Cost *$23*

The headpiece and veil are very easy to make. Several seamstresses I interviewed said that when they make the wedding gown they use leftover tulle netting to assemble a headpiece. The puffed-up, gathered, bouffant-look is popular now, and that is the easiest of all to put together.

Use a ready-made frame, whether it's a full cap, hat or narrow headband. Attach the netting and any other silk flowers, pearls or lace that you wish to add. If you find a headpiece and veil you like in a bridal shop, just buy the necessary embellishments at a fabric store and copy them. Anyone can do this, even someone who doesn't sew. This is what an elegant headpiece and veil would cost to make:

Headband	$ 7.00
Tulle lace, 2 yards, 108″ wide @ $2.98 per yard	5.96
Two silk flowers with pearl edging	5.00
Extra embellishments	5.00
Total	$22.96

Hire a Seamstress
Approximate Cost *$60*

The seamstresses I interviewed charge an average of $60 to make the headpiece and veil, including materials and labor. It can run less if it's made from the netting left over from the dress and attached to a very simple cap.

Buy Discount
Approximate Cost *$75*

Try the factory outlets and catalogs. Your Discount Bridal Service representative will also be able to help you. She can find the veil of your choice for 20 to 40 percent off the retail price. There are also several Web sites that carry reasonably priced headpieces and veils, including A La Mode and Autumn Moon Designs, plus the "Bargain Basement" at Romantic Headlines (see Resources on pages 176-179).

The Bride's Slip

If you decide to purchase a slip in a bridal salon, expect to pay between $75 and $150. This added expense can easily be avoided with these ideas:

Something Borrowed
No Cost *$0*

There are closets all over town cluttered with wedding slips, and you probably know a few of their owners. Drop a few hints here and there and you'll find that brides are glad to loan out their wedding petticoats. After our daughter had already purchased hers, she was offered two of them. You may want to wait as long as possible to make this purchase, because I'm sure one will appear. If nothing lands on your doorstep by three weeks before the wedding, go ahead and use another plan.

Rent It
Approximate Cost . . . .*$15–$20*

Most of the petticoats I saw for rent had lost their "puff." A bouffant nylon slip really doesn't hold its shape for long, so you may want to rent one only if it's fairly new and gives your gown the necessary support.

Free Seamstress
Approximate Cost *$10*

Use white sheeting or muslin fabric for the body of the slip and then add ruffles of stiff nylon netting. The number of ruffles depends upon the fullness of the wedding dress. An average petticoat will require approximately 3⅞ yards of 72-inch netting.

A very full petticoat will require 6 yards. Be sure to make the petticoat as full as necessary in order to give the skirt the support it needs.

This should be your total cost to sew your own petticoat:

Stiff nylon netting, 6 yards, 72″ @ $1.19 per yard	$ 7.14
Muslin, 2 yards, 45″ @ $.99 per yard	1.98
Thread	.89
Total	$10.01

Hire a Seamstress
Approximate Cost *$60*

A seamstress will charge approximately $50 to make the slip for you. This, added to the cost of the materials, totals $60. Whether you sew it yourself or hire a seamstress, you'll have a much sturdier petticoat than you can purchase, with all the fullness needed for your particular wedding gown.

Buy Discount
Approximate Cost *$40*

Look around for sales and bargains at the factory outlet stores. Catalog shopping is also a possibility, and don't forget to check with your Discount Bridal Service representative.

The Bride's Shoes

The bride's shoes can become another costly surprise if you don't shop wisely. As you can imagine, full retail price on her shoes can run over $100 in a bridal or shoe salon. Here are some cost-cutting suggestions:

Something Borrowed
No Cost *$0*

Perhaps you have a friend or relative who'll loan you her shoes for the wedding. Remember, they don't have to be "wedding" shoes, only the right shade of white. Be open-minded on this idea, for you may find that someone's dressy white heels might be just what you need. If you're wearing a floor-length gown, the shoe is not as important as you may think. The most important thing is that the shoe is soft and comfortable. Be sure that the heel is not too high and that the shoes are plenty roomy. They say that your wedding shoe should be one size larger than you normally wear because your feet will swell as the day goes along. You want the shoe to feel like a slipper all day so that you'll still feel fresh by the end of the reception.

Buy Discount
Approximate Cost *$20*

Inexpensive shoes can be found at Payless Shoes, Kmart, Target and other discount stores, as well as factory outlet shops. You don't need a shoe with quality that will last for years; you only need a pair that looks great and feels comfortable for about ten hours. Be sure to shop late in the day when your feet are swollen. Remember that on the day of the wedding your feet will be equally as swollen, or more so, because stress causes additional water retention. Be safe—buy big!

Buy Skimmers
Approximate Cost *$30*

A bridal "skimmer" is a slipper-type shoe in white satin. It's a very comfortable shoe and comes perfectly flat or with a tiny wedge. I highly recommend this style shoe because of its comfort and low price. It's "wobble-proof" when you walk down the aisle and will guarantee that you'll leave on your honeymoon with a "happy back." You may find that a regular ballerina slipper will accomplish this same purpose, and it may cost even less than a skimmer. Both of these slippers are very plain and can be embellished, if you like, with any number of wedding accessories available at your fabric or craft stores. There are white satin rosettes, ribbons, pearls, sequins or lace appliques, all of which can be glued on with fabric glue or a hot-glue gun.

If you're not wearing a floor-length gown, you may want to avoid such a flat shoe, but whatever shoes you choose, be sure to break them in before the wedding. Wear them around the house, covered with a big pair of socks to keep them clean. Stand in them while you do the dishes or iron. Just remember that if you ever wanted a comfortable pair of shoes, it's on your wedding day.

Note: To locate ballerina slippers, look in your local yellow pages under Dancing Supplies.

> *Tip* As this book goes to press, there is a trend toward converting a pair of comfortable, broken-in white tennis shoes into wedding shoes by embellishing with white lace, sequins, beads and appliquéd lace. What a great idea! Of course, this only works with a floor-length gown, but talk about comfort!

Now you have ideas for your gown, headpiece, slip and shoes, and at much lower costs than you thought. Don't forget to record all your ideas in the notebook under the "Clothing" section. Which plans sound good to you? Who may be able to loan you a wedding slip? Will Aunt Jenny's veil work? Put your thoughts on paper so that you don't forget them!

Have fun putting it all together—I know you'll be a beautiful bride!

4

What a Handsome Bunch!

*(Outfitting the Wedding Party
Without Breaking the Bank)*

Now that the bride is all set, we need to dress the rest of the wedding party. Very few of the expenses described in this chapter are usually borne by the bride's family, except for their own personal attire.

The rest of the bridal party, however, including the bridesmaids, junior attendants, groomsmen, flower girl and ring bearer, usually pay their own way. But just in case the bride's family will need to cover any of these expenses, this chapter offers cost-cutting ideas for each of them.

The Mother's Dress

The mother's dress should blend into the color scheme; it should not clash or stand out as some kind of fashion statement. This is not Mom's high school reunion where she wants to be the slimmest, sexiest woman in the room; this is the bride's day and Mom doesn't want to distract from the bride's gown.

The mother's dress should be somewhat conservative, and not longer or more formal than her daughter's dress. If the bride's dress is tea length or street length, the mother's dress should not be floor length. The mother's dress should be a neutral color or one that complements the bridesmaids' dresses. The style of Mom's dress should also fit in with the wedding's theme. A very contemporary dress, for example, wouldn't be appropriate for a ''Southern Antebellum'' theme.

When I went shopping for my mother-of-the-bride dress, I was appalled at many of those for sale at the bridal salons. They not only made me feel fat and old, but the prices gave me an upset stomach. Some of the dresses looked like drapes wrapped around with a pin holding them together—and they cost hundreds of dollars! I'll tell you later where I bought my dress, but it definitely was not at a bridal salon.

Here are ways for Mom to save money:

Something Borrowed
Approximate Cost **$40**

If Mom can borrow a dress, her only costs should be alterations, if required.

Rent It
Approximate Cost **$50**

You'll be delighted with the beautiful dresses available for mother at the rental shops. Some of these dresses would cost as much as $700 to purchase and yet can be rented for as little as $50.

Buy From a Resale Shop
Approximate Cost . . . . **40%–70% off retail**

Mom may luck out and find exactly what she's looking for at a resale or consignment shop. Many of these stores sell finer dresses with brand-name labels. If you live in a small town with very few shops to choose from, it might be worth it to take a drive to a larger city nearby. The trip could save you $100, or more.

Buy Discount
Approximate Cost **$40**

Believe it or not, you can buy a mother's dress at a factory outlet store for as low as $40. Also, try the catalogs and keep your eye on sales everywhere in general.

Free Seamstress
Approximate Cost **$57**

The following costs are based on a Simplicity pattern. I walked into my local fabric store and scouted out these materials at regular price. If you shop around for fabric sales, I'm sure you could cut the cost considerably.

Pattern	$14.00
Taffeta slip fabric, 1¾ yards, 45″ @ $3.99 per yard	6.98
Chiffon slip flounce, 2½ yards, 45″ @ $6.99 per yard	17.48
Dress fabric, single-edged Galloon lace, 2⅜ yards, 45″ @ $5.98 per yard	14.20

Neck facing, ⅝ yard of 54″ tulle @ $2.98 per yard		1.86
Three ⅜″ buttons @ $.50 each		1.50
	Total	$56.02

Hire a Seamstress
Approximate Cost *$157*

A seamstress will charge approximately $100 to make a mother-of-the bride dress. This, added to the cost for the materials, will give you the dress of your choice for about $157. Note: Because seamstresses' costs have gone up so much since my last revision of this book, you may do better with one of the other options.

Buy a "Finer" Dress
Approximate Cost *$150*

Go to the Finer Dresses or Special Occasion section of your local department store. You'll find styles that are more youthful and becoming, and much less expensive than most mother-of-the-bride dresses. This is where I found my dress on sale for under $50, and I received many compliments on it. The bodice was lined and appliqued with satin flowers that were sprinkled with small pearls. It had a soft, full chiffon skirt and filmy sleeves with satin cuffs. It was cream-colored and compatible with the burgundy color scheme. A soft pink, the wedding's accent color, would also have worked well.

As soon as I found my dress, by the way, I snipped a fabric sample from an inside seam and sent it, along with a photo of the dress, to the mother of the groom who lives in another city. She used this as a guide to purchase her own dress which was very similar to mine in color and style. Both of our dresses were street length.

The Bridesmaids' Dresses

Here's some free advice, worth the price of this book: "DON'T TAKE ALL THE BRIDESMAIDS SHOPPING AT THE SAME TIME!" If all the bridesmaids hop together from place to place, trying on dresses and arguing over styles, you'll not only have a wasted day, but you'll also have a mega headache.

Have you ever been in a restaurant and overheard a group of women arguing over the bill? "No, I had the tuna salad sandwich and coffee. I didn't have a salad at all. Mine should only be $5.75." "Well, I know mine won't be over $6.50 because I had the special," and so forth. It's embarrassing to watch them with their mini-calculators, haggling away. You're faced with a similar situation when the whole pack of attendants travels en masse, trying on bridesmaids' dresses.

To avoid this entire nightmarish possibility, make a plan ahead of time. Have an idea of the general style of dress you'll be looking for, taking into consideration the wedding's theme. Also, have a color family in mind. It's best not to get your heart set on an exact color because it may be difficult to find, but you can usually come very close.

Also, consider whether the women can afford to pay retail prices at a bridal salon. Would it be better to have their dresses sewn from a pattern of the bride's choice? Is it unlikely to find a ready-made style that will be flattering to each of their figures? Also, what about their finances? Even though the attendants traditionally pay for their own wedding attire, it might be helpful to suggest some cost-cutting ideas. After all, if even one of the bridesmaids is on a tight budget, it would be courteous for all of them to agree to something other than bridal salon prices. As you've probably guessed, I have a number of ways for them to save money.

Rent It
Approximate Cost *$50*

This is the least expensive plan; however, for very little more she can have the "Free Seamstress" plan or the "Buy Discount" plan and end up with a dress she can keep. The bridesmaids' dresses that are available for rent are high quality and, if the shop has them available in the color and sizes you require, this might be the best plan for your friends. Most of the shops will allow alterations.

Free Seamstress
Approximate Cost *$61*

Under this plan each attendant must arrange for her own volunteer seamstress. The attendants may all go to the fabric store together to purchase the fabric and other materials, or one person may take care of it and be reimbursed later. Here are the materials required for an average Simplicity pattern bridesmaid's dress:

Pattern	$15.00
Fabric, 8⅝ yards 45″ taffeta @ $3.99 per yard	34.41
Zipper, 22″	3.00
Thread	1.89
Two ⅜″ buttons for sleeves @ $.50 each	1.00
One lace medallion	4.00
Interfacing, ½ yard @ $2.29 per yard	1.15
Total	$60.45

You can save quite a bit on the materials by hunting for fabric sales. These are the advantages of using the "Free Seamstress" plan:

❦ *You can select the pattern of your choice* that will be flattering to all the attendants' figures.

❦ *The dresses will fit perfectly.* When ordering from a bridal salon there is the awful possibility that you discover, at the very last minute, that the dress makes one of the chubbier attendants look like Miss Piggy. When the dresses are sewn at home, the fit can be just right, even if it means making up the bodice first in sheeting fabric. This is a good idea, especially for the extra-bosomy bridesmaid. By making up the bodice in sheeting fabric first, you can see whether the neckline needs to be cut higher. Extremely sexy bridesmaids are not real popular with the bride.

❦ *You'll not have to special order the dresses* through a salon where you can't be sure that all the dresses will arrive from the manufacturer in time for the wedding. Also, you have the freedom of selecting a color and fabric of your choice. In a salon it may be difficult to find the style you want in the right color and fabric. Usually, there must be a compromise, selecting the dress that comes as close as possible to what the bride really envisioned.

Hire a Seamstress
Approximate Cost *$161*

If you have doubts about using a volunteer seamstress, you may want to have the dresses sewn by a professional. The average seamstress's fee for making a bridesmaid's dress is $100. This, added to the price of the materials, will bring the total to approximately $161. Again, most of the seamstresses I spoke with will help shop for the pattern and fabric and will arrive at the wedding ahead of time to make any last-minute alterations. A good seamstress, too, can tell you whether or not a certain style will be suitable for each of the attendants' figures, but she will need to see each woman and take measurements in order to help with this decision. Note: Because seamstresses' costs have gone up since my last revision, it may be more affordable to choose one of the other plans.

Buy Discount
Approximate Cost *$50*

Try the factory outlets for dresses suitable for a wedding. In this case, there's no escape from shopping with all the bridesmaids at once. (Bring the aspirin.) If you're lucky, you may find dresses that are alike, one in each size required. It's worth a try, in spite of the hysteria, if the attendants really need to save money. At some of the San Francisco outlets I found awesome dresses priced as low as $30. Some of the outlets, such as Gunne Sax, have actual bridesmaids' dresses at their bridal location. You may find these dresses for under $50 each.

The next best thing is to try the mail-order catalogs. This is what my daughter did. She selected a dress out of the JCPenney catalog that happened to be perfect in color, fabric and style. The dress was two-piece with a peplum jacket and elegant shirred sleeves. The fabric was a shiny polyester that looked like heavy satin. The color was exactly right—burgundy. She was able to see an actual sample of the fabric at a JCPenney's bridal salon at a local mall.

Her bridesmaids were scattered: one in Denver, one in San Francisco, one in Fresno and one in our hometown. Each bridesmaid took her own measurements, which determined the size that should be ordered. Then our daughter ordered all of the dresses at one time from the same lot, to be delivered to each girl at her local JCPenney's store. Each bridesmaid paid for her own dress when she picked it up. It worked great. These dresses were on sale for $60 each and, without the jacket, were quite practical for each girl to wear later, especially when hemmed to street length.

We later saw this *identical* dress, by the way, for sale in a bridal salon for $270!

You may also want to take a look at a few Web sites: www.chadwicks.com, www.bestbridesmaid.com and www.bestpromdresses.com. Each of these Web sites sells affordable prom and special occasion gowns that will also serve as bridesmaids' gowns.

Note: JCPenney's carries bridesmaids' gowns in their bridal party catalog, located in their Special Occasion section of their local stores.

Bridesmaids' Headpieces

Free Seamstress
Approximate Cost $2

The bridesmaids' headpieces can be made for practically nothing. I made them for my daughter's wedding at a cost of under $1 each. Luckily, one of the bridesmaids was only about five feet tall and we had a good foot of fabric left over when she had her dress shortened, enough to make four large, flat bows, lined with stiffening from the fabric store. Attached to these bows was gathered burgundy netting that hung to shoulder-length. Where the netting met the bow I added two burgundy silk rosettes and white baby's breath. You don't have to be a seamstress or especially "crafty" to come up with something like this. Just look at the bridesmaids' headpieces for sale in salons or modeled in bridal magazines and duplicate them at home.

Flowers and Ribbon
Approximate Cost $4

If you don't want any fuss at all, tie one or two fresh or silk flowers with a piece of satin ribbon that matches the dress. The bridesmaids can wear these on the side or back of their heads.

Hat Plus
> *Approximate Cost* *$10*

If a hat is the perfect accessory, buy an inexpensive one from a craft store or discount department store; they're often available for under $5. Spray-paint it in the right color and embellish it with all the goodies of your choice—ribbons, rosettes, baby's breath or fabric. Be original—anything goes! (Note: Spray paint works well on cloth and straw hats but don't try it on vinyl or leather, as it will crack.)

Bridesmaids' Slips
Wear Your Own
> *No Cost* *$0*

Most women have a slip that will work, unless the dress requires one that is quite full, in which case she will need to use another plan.

Something Borrowed
> *No Cost* *$0*

She can borrow a slip that has been used by either a bride or a bridesmaid.

Rent It
> *Approximate Cost* . . . . *$10–$25*

This is a very practical way to go, but it will depend on your proximity to a good rental shop. It may not be worth the drive just to rent a slip.

Free Seamstress
> *Approximate Cost* . . . . *$10–$25*

The materials will cost the same or a little less than for the bride's slip.

Hire a Seamstress
> *Approximate Cost* *$60*

Again, the cost for materials and labor will be about the same or a little less than for the bride.

Bridesmaids' Shoes
Wear Their Own
> *No Cost* *$0*

Dyed-to-match pumps are no longer expected. It has become quite acceptable for the bridesmaids to wear their own shoes. Of course, all the shoes should be of the same general color, height and style. Women generally have a plain pump that will work with most dresses. If the dress is floor-length, it's really easy to get away with wearing their own shoes. The height of the heel and style of the shoes won't matter; only the color should be the same, and the shoes should be polished and in good repair. Of course, the flatter the shoe, the more comfortable.

Buy Discount
Approximate Cost ***$20***

If it's necessary to purchase shoes, go for the most inexpensive you can find. A recent Los Angeles bride found perfect matching pumps for her bridesmaids at Target on sale for $9.99 a pair. (This was after finding their dresses at a Lanz outlet in mid-Wilshire at $45 apiece.) Just be sure they are comfortable and a size larger than normal. The bridesmaids don't want pinched toes either.

Buy Skimmers
Approximate Cost ***$25***

Follow the same advice given the bride. A flat, ballerina-style shoe or slipper can be the ultimate in comfort. This is especially practical when worn with a floor-length dress.

The Flower Girl's Dress

A dress for a flower girl or junior attendant can cost as much as $150 when purchased at a bridal salon or children's shop. Outfitting these little gals can dig deep into their parents' food budget for the month, and, unfortunately, the rental shops usually don't carry dresses below women's size 6. But don't despair—there are several ways around this dilemma.

Embellish Her Party Dress
Approximate Cost ***$5***

Most little girls have a special "party dress." It may be a confirmation dress or Easter dress. If you're lucky, like my daughter was, it may be in white or a color that will work in the wedding. My daughter's little niece happened to have a pale pink party dress with a full skirt. She even had her own matching "Mary Jane" shoes. All the dress needed to coordinate with the wedding colors was a big sash, which was easily obtained. Her head was topped with a wreath of flowers, and she looked adorable as she walked down the aisle carrying the basket of flowers.

The sash can be made out of fabric or ribbon of the same color as the bridesmaids' dresses. If you purchase this fabric or ribbon, it will cost about $3; if you have scraps left over from the bridesmaids' dresses, it will be free.

Free Seamstress
Approximate Cost *$35*

If the dress can be sewn by a volunteer, here is what you can expect to pay for the materials. These costs are based on a Simplicity pattern:

Pattern	$14.00
Fabric, 3⅛ yards, 45″ taffeta @ $3.99 per yard	12.47
Sash, 2 yards, 1½″ wide @ $2.00 per yard	4.00
Thread	1.89
Zipper, 12″	2.60
Total	$34.96

One distinct advantage of making the dress is that it can match the bridesmaids' dresses, if that is what you want. The pattern books have flower girl and junior attendant patterns that coordinate with wedding dresses and bridesmaids' dresses.

Hire a Seamstress
Approximate Cost *$85*

Professional seamstresses charge approximately $50 to make a flower girl's or junior attendant's dress. This, added to the cost of the materials, brings the total to approximately $85, which is getting up there in price, so you may want to consider one of the other plans.

Buy Discount
Approximate Cost *$30*

Shop around the discount stores, catalogs and look for sales. Resale shops are a good bet as well.

Men's Attire

When a friend or relative of the groom agrees to be a groomsman or usher in the wedding, it's an unspoken understanding that he will pay to rent his own tuxedo. If it will be very difficult for one of the men to handle this expense, it's courteous for the groom to offer to pay for it himself.

As we all know, the designer tuxes can run up there in cost, not including the shoes, which can rent for an additional $25 or so. Fortunately there are discount tuxedo rentals available that range from $40 to $95, depending on where you live; these tuxedos are usually copies of the more expensive designer brands.

By the way, many tuxedo rental companies offer the groom's rental for free if all the groomsmen rent their tuxedos from the shop. Also, look for a rental company that also offers alterations and free delivery to and from the wedding site.

The style of the men's tuxedos is determined by the bride's gown. The groom's is usually distinctive from those of the groomsmen. My son-in-law, for example, wore a black tuxedo with tails; his groomsmen wore the same tuxedo, but with a short jacket. The staffs in tuxedo rental shops are helpful in making these decisions and should be consulted as soon as possible. The actual tuxedo rentals can be reserved six months before the wedding, but usually no later than one month ahead of time.

Often, the men will rent their tuxedo outfits, but wear their own shoes, saving that cost at least. I only have one alternative to renting.

Wear Their Own
No Cost $0

An inexpensive option for the men is to have them all wear dark suits. You'll be amazed how uniform they will look, especially when wearing their boutonnieres. If one of the men only has a light-colored suit, find a darker one that he can borrow.

Another alternative, especially if it's an outdoor wedding, is to wear a navy blazer over white, cream or beige trousers; most men already have blazers hanging in their closets, but if they need to purchase them, they'll be practical additions to any man's wardrobe. The father of the bride, by the way, usually wears the same attire as the groomsmen, but the groom's father has the choice of wearing the same attire as the bride's father or wearing a dark suit instead. The bride and groom need to be sensitive to the financial capabilities of the men who have been asked to participate in the wedding. If even one of the men will suffer a financial hardship by renting an outfit, it can be courteous to suggest this alternative.

I don't recommend, however, having the groom wear a tuxedo while his grooms-men wear dark suits. The contrast will be too great. If the men in the party wear their own suits, so must the groom.

> **Tip** There is a trend toward purchasing used tuxedos from a tuxedo rental shop for about $100 to $150. That way each man has a tuxedo in his closet for his next formal affair.

Ring Bearer and Boy Attendants

The cost of renting a little tux, plus shoes, bow tie and cummerbund can run close to that of the men's. A little boy looks very cute in a miniature tuxedo, but he can be equally darling for much less money. Here are some ideas:

Wear His Own
Approximate Cost *$4*

If you're lucky, your little guy may have his own suit. All you'll need to provide is a bow tie to coordinate with the wedding colors. It's acceptable, by the way, for the ring bearer to wear his own suit even though the men are wearing tuxedos. If the ring bearer is really young, he can wear a pair of white shorts with a white dress shirt, embellished with a bow tie. When he carries the ring pillow down the aisle, your guests won't notice what he's wearing as much as how cute he looks as he walks and smiles. Luckily, a child doesn't need expensive clothes to be a precious addition to the wedding party.

Buy Discount
Approximate Cost *$50*

For less than the cost of renting a tuxedo, the boy's parents can purchase a complete outfit. This way the child will be able to wear the clothes again. Watch for sales at children's shops, shop discount stores and mail-order catalogs, and don't forget to check out resale shops that handle children's clothing!

If the wedding party uses the money-saving ideas in this chapter, they'll be relieved of much of what can be a real financial burden. This will also be a great relief to you as you plan your wedding, knowing that no one had to skip a car payment to serve as a member of your wedding party.

5

Would a Rose by Any Other Name . . . ?

(Beautiful Flowers on a Budget)

They say you can't fool all of the people all of the time. Not true! You can—especially when it comes to the flowers.

We're going to have so much fun in this chapter. I'll give you dozens of ways to fool people. In fact, you'll have a hard time keeping a straight face when they rave on, "My, you really splurged on the flowers. You must have spent a fortune." You'll humbly thank them, of course, while saying to yourself, "I'll never let them know we only spent $206 on all the flowers combined."

Yes, it *is* possible to spend as little as only $206 on everything, including a sanctuary full of flowers, twenty-five corsages and boutonnieres, the bridal bouquet, five attendants' bouquets, flower girl's basket and all the extra special things you only hoped to afford. I'll tell you how. Just remember that you can never have too many flowers and there is certainly no reason to scrimp.

I went to a wedding once where money was a real problem and they did scrimp. Unfortunately, it really showed. There were no flowers in the church at all and each bridesmaid carried a single daisy. The bride had a nice little bouquet and the groom had a rose in his lapel, but the rest of the men wore no boutonnieres at all. They had obviously decided that the flowers were a good place to cut costs, but they didn't realize the importance of flowers at a wedding. A wedding without flowers feels like a day in traffic court—there just isn't a festive atmosphere.

Flowers have traditionally been an important part of the wedding ceremony. They denote celebration and congratulation; they fill the room with joy! You must have flowers, and as many as you can afford. And you'll find that you can afford a lot more than you originally thought after reading this chapter.

First of all, you need to know what wedding flowers cost these days. The average amount spent on a wedding nationally is approximately $1,000, and even higher in large metropolitan cities, so you'll be interested in what this chapter has to offer in the way of economical alternatives.

By the way, a basic professional wedding package usually includes the following:

- ❦ One bridal bouquet in colonial, arm bouquet or cascade design

- ❦ Attendants' bouquets in a colonial style or arm bouquet for one maid of honor and three bridesmaids

- ❦ Two mothers' corsages

- ❦ Four grandmothers' corsages

- ❦ Twelve boutonnieres

- ❦ Two altar arrangements

- ❦ Flower girl basket

Of course, you'll also want more than the basic package, such as arrangements for the reception, corsages for your guest book attendants, and corsage and boutonniere for the reception host and hostess. But don't despair, because there are clever ways to have lots of flowers without breaking the bank.

The first plan will save you the most money, but even if it isn't feasible to "borrow" all the flowers, you may be able to cut costs by having at least some of them donated.

Free Florist
Approximate Cost *$206*

All the flowers and greenery you can use are waiting to be donated or loaned. There are people out there who can hardly wait to provide everything you need—for free!

Private gardens are full of flowers, shrubs, evergreens, ferns and flowering bushes. And the best news is that these gardens belong to your friends, relatives and local garden club members who are notoriously generous people. Their lovely flowers are just waiting for your approval. In fact, people with green thumbs are some of the nicest I know and they feel honored that anyone wants to show off their flowers in a wedding.

If you're brave, you might even knock on neighbors' doors if you see something in their yards that would be helpful. You may find that they not only offer you cut flowers but will gladly haul out their ladders and pruning shears to cut down branches of their blooming dogwood trees. Of course, for a good part of the country in the dead of winter there will only be a few things available, such as evergreen boughs or pyracantha berries. But people will often offer baskets, vases, indoor plants, trellises and other decorative items as well.

It may surprise you that people get so mushy over weddings, but even the hardest heart seems to soften at the thought of the loving couple. It also doesn't hurt to look as pitiful as possible when you ask for help!

Another ingenious source of free flowers is to plant them yourself in your own garden, to be "harvested" a day or so before the wedding. This way you'll have the exact type and quantity of flower you need.

Your local nursery is another wonderful source of free plants, shrubs and trees. They'll sometimes loan a certain number of their plants at no charge. We borrowed fifteen huge potted evergreen trees for our daughter's reception that turned the hall into a winter wonderland. As long as we returned the trees undamaged, there was no cost to us at all.

If your wedding is planned for the spring or summer, keep your eyes open for fields of wildflowers; these flowers add an interesting and delicate touch to the corsages. They can also be used to make up massive arrangements for the reception. Watch for delights such as Queen Anne's Lace, black-eyed Susans, daisies, asters and goldenrod. Be sure to shake out any little critters who may have made these flowers their home.

The church or synagogue itself can also be a source of free flowers, particularly if the wedding is planned for a time when it's already decorated for another reason. For example, our daughter's wedding was in December when the church had a twenty-five-foot tree covered with tiny white lights, railings draped with garlands of flowers and pillars dripping with ribboned evergreen sprays.

These are some of the flowers normally used for weddings: roses, spider mums, carnations, orchids, lilacs, daisies, asters, bells of Ireland, lilies, stephanotis and baby's breath. But be open-minded to anything you see that is growing. You don't have to use traditional flowers; be creative—try something unusual. You may be interested to know that there are florists who win awards for their wedding arrangements because of their creative uses of nontraditional flowers. These florists are even employed by the "rich and famous" to come up with something different. People are trying to get away from the same old thing. So, look upon free flowers with great glee, and if they don't win you an award, just let me know and I'll send you one!

I'm assuming you'll be able to borrow all the baskets and vases you'll need, so your only cost will be the supplies listed below. These can be purchased from a floral supply store.

SUPPLIES	COST
Acetate ribbon, 100 yards, 1½″ wide	$ 29.00
Acetate ribbon, 100 yards, 3″ wide	53.00
Acetate ribbon, 100 yards, ⅝″ wide	16.60
Satin ribbon for streamers, 8 yards	5.28
Florist wire, three boxes	12.00
Florist tape, 60 yards	4.50

Plastic bouquet holder, six	11.94
Ready-made corsage forms, four	12.00
Corsage pins, two packages	2.00
Net, ½ yard, 6″ wide	3.00
Stemmed corsage inserts (pearls, rosettes, etc.)	4.00
Tablecloth lace, ½ yard	4.50
Other corsage embellishments (satin leaves, etc.)	10.00
Baby's breath, two sprays	12.00
Stardust Gypsy, two sprays	8.40
Forty small silk flowers such as lilies of the valley, stephanotis, bells of Ireland, etc.	18.00
Total	$206.22

Note: A user-friendly, no-fail bow maker is also available for about $10, if you're short on time and need to create dozens of bows quickly.

When you're at the floral supply store, ask for a free demonstration in making corsages, bouquets, and bows. This is what I did and was surprised at how easy it is to learn. They even have bouquets and corsages made up for you to see as examples. Later you can use brides' magazines and florists' brochures for ideas. But don't forget the importance of being original, too.

The folks at the floral supply will show you the easy way to make the bride's and attendants' bouquets by using a plastic bouquet holder as a base. It has a handle that fastens to a doilied cup with hidden oasis, the damp block that holds the flowers firmly in place while keeping them watered. Just insert the flower stems into the oasis, along with some trailing ribbons or some ivy.

The same is true for the corsages. You'll learn to use the wire and tape to hold the flowers in place. It's so much fun you may be tempted to open your own flower shop (well, maybe not, but the thought may cross your mind!). You'll only need to use the ready-made forms for the larger corsages; the rest will be fine with ribbon, greenery and other embellishments added; they should be made up the day before the wedding and refrigerated.

The last seven items on the supply list can be used to give the bouquets and corsages that professional look. The tablecloth lace is to be cut up into lace strips, saving the cost of buying lace by the yard. Cut the lace into whatever widths you need. Make full loops of lace two or three inches wide for the bouquets, or very narrow strips to place on top of the ribbon in the corsages.

The narrow satin ribbon should be used only for the streamers in the bouquets and flower girl basket. Tie several knots in these streamers; it helps them hang nicely. Acetate ribbon will not work because it won't tie into these pretty love knots.

The men's boutonnieres are the simplest of all to make. Use a single flower, usually

Styles of Bouquets

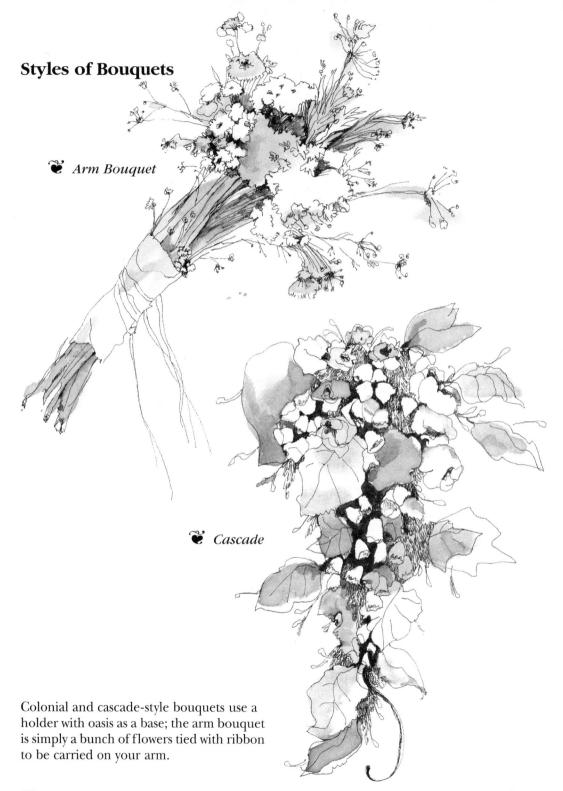

🍂 *Arm Bouquet*

🍂 *Cascade*

Colonial and cascade-style bouquets use a holder with oasis as a base; the arm bouquet is simply a bunch of flowers tied with ribbon to be carried on your arm.

a tight rosebud, and wrap the stem with florist's tape, working in something delicate and white, such as baby's breath. You don't even need a ribbon for these, so they make up very quickly.

You can't go wrong on the flower girl's basket—just be sure it isn't too large and has a handle. Fill it with flowers or fresh rose petals and trail some of the satin ribbon. Wire a few of the same flowers together to make a wreath or hairpiece; add some ribbon and baby's breath, and she'll look adorable.

After you've assembled and refrigerated the bouquets, boutonnieres and the flower girl's basket, start decorating the church and reception hall. You'll need to transport boxes full of flowers, greenery and supplies, including scissors, tape, etc. When you arrive at the church to do your decorating, you'll feel confident because you'll have so much to work with. That is the way it is with the "free florist"—you don't need to scrimp. Just be sure to have plenty of volunteers so you won't feel pressured.

With the clergyman's permission, attach flowers, greenery and ribbon to the pews, windows, pillars, candelabra, altar tables and the tops of the organ and piano. Use a little watered oasis to keep everything fresh throughout the wedding, except for the evergreen boughs which are hardy and need no help. Make garlands for doorways and staircases by wiring greenery and ribbon together. You would need a bank loan to pay a professional florist for all these extras.

The same is true in the reception hall. You'll have plenty of flowers and greenery to decorate walls, doorways, arches, trellises, tables, the cake, punch bowl, and cake knife. Since cost is not a factor, you can go wild.

If you run out of a certain color flower while you're decorating the church and hall, do what florists sometimes do—spray paint some tufts of greenery to fill in. I suggest that you have a small can of spray paint on hand just in case this happens; buy it in your primary wedding color.

You'll find many advantages to the "free florist" plan. The main advantage, of course, is that it's the least expensive way to go. Another is the great sense of satisfaction in the creativity. Every corsage will be special and unique. The baskets of flowers will be unlike any your guests have ever seen. After all, the same florists have probably been doing the weddings in your town for years—it's definitely time for some originality.

Obviously, one of the greatest advantages is that you'll be able to have more flowers and larger arrangements than you could have afforded otherwise. How else can you provide all those extra corsages, the garlands along the banisters and the pew flowers? There's no doubt you'll need to supply smelling salts for those guests who swoon at your opulence!

One of the nicest things about this plan, too, is the fun your volunteers will have putting it all together. It can be a real party in itself. You may have had doubts about their artistic capabilities, but you'll be surprised how easily it all goes together. There's something exhilarating about converting piles of flowers and supplies into beautiful works of art. Be sure that you've used your notebook to keep track of these volunteers, as well as those who provided flowers. You'll want to thank them for their kindness.

There are a couple of disadvantages to the plan, however. If you live in a big city,

How to Make a Garland

Cut your greenery to a uniform length—eight to twelve inches is good. Bunch several lengths of greenery in your hand, then wrap them with florist wire, leaving some wire hanging. Add another clump of greens so that it overlaps the first, and reinforce it with wire. Continue adding bunches and wrapping with florist wire until the garland reaches the desired length.

Add fresh flowers at the last minute, once the garland is in place. (Garlands can be made a day or two ahead—simply mist and place them in plastic bags punched with holes. Store in a cool place, if possible.)

there aren't as many gardens, so you'll need to arrange with your country friends and relatives to bring their cuttings to you a few days before the wedding. Just be sure to cut the stems *under water* so they'll keep until you'll be using them. This prevents air pockets from forming and will force intake of water into the stalks. They'll stay fresh for several days this way.

This plan also has a distinct disadvantage to the bride who'll be having a winter wedding in a northern state. It will be difficult to find anything blooming at that time of year. One solution is the old spray-paint trick—"make" flowers out of certain shrubs and greenery. Otherwise, the winter bride may want to use silk flowers as explained in the next money-saving plan.

Fool Them With Silks
Approximate Cost *$364*

This plan is similar to the "Free Florist" plan except that you'll use silk flowers in place of fresh. You'll still need some filler foliage from your yard or florist and the same supplies from the floral supply store.

There are hundreds of silk flowers to choose from. They'll average about $.72 per flower. Just be picky and select only those flowers that look exactly like the real thing. Here is a sampling of silk flower prices with the column price indicating how much *each* individual flower costs. By the way, whenever you can, *always* buy a spray of flowers instead of single stems. A spray has a number of flowers on small stems that shoot off a main stem.

Rose, hand-wrapped (eight roses per spray)	$ 1.00
Carnations, miniature (six carnations per spray)	.53
Carnations, large (twelve carnations per spray)	.68
Gypsophila, six sprigs	.73
Orchids, the highest quality and most realistic	5.00
Daisies, medium (twenty per bush)	.25
Gardenias, highest quality and most realistic	2.50
Larkspur, tall	2.00

Your costs may be slightly more or less, depending on the flowers you select and how close you live to a large import outlet. Here is one case where big-city brides have an advantage—the larger the city, the better your prices on silk flowers and floral supplies are likely to be.

If you don't live near a big city, it may be worth the trip for the money you'll save, as well as the selection. The residents of the smaller towns in northern California shop the discount market in San Francisco all the time.

Now that you have an idea of the prices, here is an actual budget for a wedding done in silk flowers. I have listed everything you'll need.

Bride's bouquet, twenty flowers @ $.75 ea.	$ 15.00
Attendants' bouquets, fifteen flowers @ $.75 ea.	11.25
Flower girl's basket, fifteen flowers @ $.75 ea.	11.25
Boutonnieres, fifteen single roses @ $.59 ea.	8.85
Two mothers' corsages, orchids, @ $5 ea.	10.00
Four grandmothers' corsages, five flowers ea. (roses or miniature carnations) @ $.59 ea.	11.80
Ten other corsages, two carnations per corsage @ $.69 ea.	13.80
Two baskets of tall altar flowers, such as larkspur, forty-eight flowers @ $.78 ea.	37.44
Pew flowers, two per pew × twenty pews @ $.59 ea.	23.60
One low table arrangement of miniature carnations for reception, thirty flowers @ $.50 ea.	15.00
Subtotal	$157.99
Plus supplies, as listed in the "Free Florist" plan	$206
Total	$363.99

Once you've purchased the silk flowers and supplies, put them together following the same procedures described in the "Free Florist" plan, but first, rip the silk flowers from their stems and glue them back onto the stems or branches, so they're secure. This is especially important with boutonnieres—you don't want the single flower to fall off during the wedding, leaving just a stem.

There are two terrific advantages to this silk flower plan. One is that you can make up the flowers ahead of time. This means you won't have to worry that Aunt Minnie got lost driving to your house with her prize roses or that someone's camellias got pelted by a hailstorm. Another plus is that you and your volunteers won't feel as rushed the day before the wedding.

The main disadvantage is that you won't have fresh flowers at the wedding. Some people actually prefer silk flowers, but, if this is a problem for you, why not order a few things from the florist? A nice choice would be the bride's bouquet and the mothers' corsages. This will add a little expense, but you'll still be saving a great deal of money by doing the rest of the wedding in silks.

> *Tip* Check out Michaels arts and crafts stores for real bargains when it comes to premade silk flower bouquets; you may find exactly what

you want for less than $15 each. They'll also be happy to work with you on custom designed silk flower bouquets and corsages, costing you up to 75 percent less than fresh flower bouquets purchased through a retail florist.

Fool Them With the Real Thing
Approximate Cost *$700*

With this plan you'll need to purchase fresh flowers from a wholesale flower mart. The costs vary only slightly throughout the United States and here, again, the big-city bride has the advantage because the best wholesale markets are in the large cities. You can find them by looking under ''Florists'' in your Business-to-Business yellow pages.

In some parts of the country, wholesale flower marts may not be open to the public. If this is the case in your town, look for a florist who'll work with you to keep costs down. For instance, some florists will sell you bunches of flowers at substantially reduced rates if you do the arranging yourself. (In effect, the retail florist acts as a wholesaler, eliminating the service expense.) Also, if you know what kinds of flowers and colors you want, but are willing to remain flexible, a florist may be able to give you a special deal at the last minute—just wait to see what's on sale the week of the wedding. I've found supermarket floral departments to be the easiest to work with—just ask them to purchase flowers for you in bulk, to be available for pickup on a certain date.

By the way, if your wedding is in the spring, you may be able to purchase armloads of peach, apple, almond or cherry blossoms directly from orchard owners at a very low cost.

Enough fresh flowers for an average wedding will cost between $450 and $550. You'll also need the same supplies mentioned in the first two plans. This will bring your total cost to between about $650 and $750.

The main advantage of this plan is that you'll have fresh flowers. One disadvantage is that you or someone dependable will have to transport the flowers from your nearest wholesale mart at the last minute. Another disadvantage is that you and your volunteers must make them up the day before the wedding, using the same procedure as the ''Free Florist'' plan.

> *Tip* If you don't live near a wholesale floral mart, check out some of the wholesale florists on the web, such as www.flowersales.com and www.codwholesale.com. Some sites also offer dynamite prices on ribbon and other floral supplies.

> *Tip* Check with a local horticultural school to see if their students will arrange your fresh flowers for a nominal fee.

Tip Consider those inexpensive potted plants (daffodils, tulips or other seasonal plant) available at The Home Depot, Target, Wal-Mart or your local supermarket. They're often available for less than $5 each and they make delightful fresh flower table centerpieces.

Supermarket Wedding Package
Approximate Cost *$400*

The supermarket chains not only bake wedding cakes in their bakeries and prepare reception food in their deli departments, but also offer lovely, affordable floral packages. Call several in your own hometown to compare plans, but to give you an idea of what you can get for the money, here's a sample wedding floral package available from a supermarket in my hometown for a total cost of $320 (mini-carnations); $410 (seasonal flowers); or $470 (roses). Here is what each of these floral packages includes:

- ❦ One Bridal Bouquet
- ❦ One Maid-of-Honor Bouquet
- ❦ Two Bridesmaids' Bouquets
- ❦ Two Corsages
- ❦ Four Boutonnieres
- ❦ One Throwaway Bridal Bouquet

Note: You can order additional bouquets, corsages, boutonnieres or arrangements at comparable prices.

Share the Joy

Sharing the joy means that two brides go together to share the cost of the professional florist's wedding package. It seems that this would save each bride a great deal of money, but remember that only the church and reception flowers can be shared. It would be a little tacky to take back corsages and boutonnieres that have been given as gifts. And since only one-third of the cost is for the church and reception flowers, that is the amount that would be split between two brides. In order to find another bride, you'll need to ask around or watch the engagement announcements in your local newspaper.

This means that each bride would save approximately one-half of the one-third, or 17 percent of the total cost.

The advantage here, of course, is the money savings. A disadvantage is that someone may have to transport the flowers from one site to another; there would also need to be a compatible color scheme.

Timing is everything in this scenario. There needs to be plenty of time to transport the flowers from the first site to the second site. Of course, if both weddings are at the same site, this simplifies things. Sharing wedding flowers usually works best when there is one sanctuary decorated in white (or a neutral color) that can be used for two weddings in one day, one in the morning and the other in the late afternoon or evening.

Rent the Showpieces

Here's an interesting idea: Whether you use silk flowers or wholesale flowers, rent the larger floral baskets or arrangements for the church and reception. The rental prices vary, but an average seems to be in this range:

Two large baskets of gladiolus and mums—$65/pair

You'll also find the bride's and attendants' bouquets for rent, but the ones I looked at seemed very "used." The larger arrangements are in better condition and worthy of consideration; rental stores carry various types of arrangements from roses to dogwood. The most common, however, seem to be baskets of glads and mums.

You may also want to consider renting six-foot pew candlesticks which will add an extremely elegant and dramatic look to the sanctuary. Decorate these tall candlesticks with ribbon, tulle netting or trailing silk, live ivy and any silk or live flowers of your choice.

The Combination Plan

With this plan, you order some of the flowers from a florist; the rest you assemble yourself. Order only the following from the florist:

❦ Bride's bouquet

❦ Attendants' bouquets

❦ Boutonnieres

❦ Flower girl's basket

❦ Corsages

All the church and reception flowers will be on the "Free Florist" plan.

This "Combination Plan" is what worked best for our daughter's wedding. We used the church's decorations, free trees at the reception and pine boughs where we could. No one needed smelling salts, but we did receive many compliments. Our total cost was $289. The advantages of this plan are the cost savings and the small amount of work at the last minute.

Tip If you do decide to purchase some of your flowers from a retail florist, you can still save money by avoiding out-of-season or exotic flowers and going with seasonal or locally-grown flowers. You can also save on the bride's and bridesmaids' bouquets by opting for affordable alternatives, included at the end of this chapter.

Floral Advice

I hope one of these plans will work for you and help save you money. And are you remembering your notebook? You should be making note of the plans that appeal to you and any sources of flowers, offers from volunteers, or prices that you may accumulate along the way. Meanwhile, whatever way you go, here are a few tidbits of advice:

- If the bride is tall, she should carry a cascading bouquet; if she is short, she needs a smaller one.

- The bride can carry a Bible or prayer book in place of a bouquet. Just place a flower on top with some white satin ribbon streamers.

- Attendants' bouquets should be smaller and more colorful than the bride's and the maid or matron of honor's bouquet should be a little larger than the other attendants'.

- If a church has a high ceiling, use tall altar flowers; if the church has a low ceiling, use a low arrangement.

- If a wedding is at night, use white flowers. Dark colors get lost in the shadows and soft lighting.

- Both mothers' corsages should be the same to avoid any hard feelings.

- If you use the "Free Florist" plan, pick the flowers slightly closed so they won't be too full on the wedding day; be especially careful to select "tight" rosebuds.

- If you find some used silk flowers that need a lift, just shake them in a bag with salt. They'll revive and look like new.

- If you decide to decorate the aisle pews, save money by decorating only the first three or four rows, which are where the family members usually sit, or decorate every third or fourth pew, instead of every one.

❦ Whatever plan you choose, you can also save money by transporting the larger floral arrangements from the ceremony site to the reception site. You can also decorate the bride's table or cake table at the reception by placing the bride's and bridesmaids' bouquets on the front of the table. Both of these ideas will help dress up the reception venue at no extra cost.

❦ Don't forget that you can always use helium-filled balloons as bouquets, in place of floral bouquets, and you can also use balloons as "filler," which will cut down on your total floral costs.

❦ Instead of flowers, use only tulle netting and ribbon for your pew decorations, which will save quite a bit, depending on how many pews you plan to decorate.

❦ When you've chosen the floral plan that best suits your budget, be sure to outline it in your notebook. Then record each expense.

Note: You may want to consider these cost-cutting alternatives to the traditional bouquet for the bride or her attendants.

❦ *Hand-Tied Nosegay*
Six to eight blooms with only six inches of stalk, tied simply with two trailing ribbons.

❦ *Hand-Tied Arm Bouquet*
This is one of the easiest and more affordable ideas of all: take a spray of fresh flowers, tie the stems together with a single wide ribbon.

❦ *Tussie-Mussie Bouquet*
This dainty option works well for a country or Victorian wedding: hand-tie a cluster of dried flowers with ribbons and insert them into a silver, cone-shaped tussie mussie (available at your floral supply store).

❦ *A White Fan Decorated With Flowers*
Purchase a ready-made lace, paper or bamboo fan that can be covered with white satin and lace and then embellished with a single flower, such as an orchid. Or, trail narrow satin ribbons or glue white pearl beads randomly over the satin and lace.

❦ *Round or Heart-Shaped Wreath*
Decorate Styrofoam or grapevine wreaths with lace, bows and trail-

ing ribbons. Add a ten-inch loop of fabric or ribbon at the top of the wreath to be slipped over the wrist.

❦ *Decorated Candy Cane*
If you're having a Christmas wedding, decorate a giant candy cane with holly, mistletoe, sprigs of evergreens, silk stephanotis, white gypsophila, plus ribbon sprinkled with "gold dust" or "white snow" sparkles.

❦ *White Fur Muff*
For any winter wedding, but especially one with a Christmas theme, create fur muffs from white rabbit fur or fake fur fabric; decorate them with a miniature nosegay or a single flower, plus narrow trailing ribbons.

❦ *Sheaves of Wheat*
Borrow from the pure simplicity of an early Roman wedding and carry a sheaf of wheat tied with a single fabric ribbon. This idea works beautifully with a Greco-Roman or Medieval theme, especially when the bridal attendants wear authentic costumes. It also works with an informal, simple outdoor wedding where the bride's and her attendants' dresses are sewn from natural fabrics, such as cotton or wool.

Isn't saving money fun? I know it's exciting for you to plan the flowers for your own special wedding, and I hope my research has helped you out. Let me know if anyone swoons.

6

What's Cookin'?

(Fabulous Food for Pennies per Person)

I know that your niece's reception at the Hotel Ritz cost $28,000 and your friend's catered garden reception cost $15,000, but I've done the research and there are wonderful ways to throw a great party for a fraction of those outrageous costs. Nationwide, wedding receptions average about $10,000 (50 percent of the total cost of the wedding).

First of all, have you set the time of the wedding? According to our calendar, one of the first duties is to set the date and location of the wedding. But if you haven't selected the time of day as yet, you may want to give this some thought: the time of the wedding can dictate the cost of the reception food. Here are some guidelines:

Morning wedding ....Continental breakfast or
(before 11 A.M.) breakfast buffet

Midday wedding ....Luncheon buffet
(11 A.M. to 1 P.M.)

Afternoon wedding ....Hors d'oeuvres buffet or
(1 to 4 P.M.) cake and punch only

Early evening wedding ......Dinner buffet
(4 to 7 P.M.)

Evening wedding ....Hors d'oeuvres buffet or
(after 7 P.M.) cake and punch only

Obviously, an afternoon or evening wedding will require the least expense in the way of food, but whatever time of day you've chosen, there are a variety of ways to feed your guests on much less than the national norm. I have several plans for you, but it's important to note that each one requires that you have control over your reception venue. In other words, it's imperative that you book a site that allows you to bring in your own food, beverages, servers, cake-cutters, cleanup crew, and so forth. The problem with so many sites, especially resorts, private clubs or hotels, is that they usually require that you order the reception food and beverages off their "special wedding menu" (including the wedding cake) and pay their servers, bartenders, cake-cutters, cleanup crews and parking valets, if they have them. So, obviously, the key is to have total control of the reception site—if you decide to bring in your own reasonably-priced caterer, fine. Fortunately, the sites that give you control are usually the most affordable venues to begin with (see chapter ten for venue ideas).

Once you have safely reserved a site that gives you control, you'll be ready to consider my economy plans. They include foods that are inexpensive and easy to prepare, even by the most mediocre cook. For all you fabulous cooks out there who like to play Emeril Lagasse on weekends, you'll find that these uncomplicated menus will be a welcome relief, especially as the day approaches. All the food is attractive and delicious and guaranteed to make your guests happy. If the guests are rude enough to ask where the food came from, just say, "Oh, it was prepared by many loving hands." They don't need to know whose.

The starred items on the following menu plans are foods that can be prepared and frozen ahead of time. Be sure to prepare and freeze ahead any foods that you can, up to six months in advance of the wedding. Keep track of these preparations in your notebook. They'll undoubtedly be stored in the freezers of friends and relatives all over town, so you'll need to keep a nice, neat list of what is where. The more you can accomplish in the weeks before the wedding, the more effortless it will seem on the big day.

By the way, whenever I mention "wholesale food suppliers," I'm referring to those food stores that not only sell to restaurants and catering services, but the general public as well. The food is of superior quality and prices are a fraction of those at your local supermarket. Many of my friends, in fact, purchase all their family foods from a wholesaler. You find the same name brands you are used to, but in bulk. All the prices are in addition to the wedding cake, which is covered later in this chapter.

Cost-Cutting Plans for the Reception Food

The Family Plan
Cost. . . . . *$.73/person, $219/300 guests*

Family members not only prepare all the food for the reception, but pay for it as well. This is the way wedding receptions were usually handled in the "olden days," but, unfortunately, this old-fashioned generosity is not seen as frequently these days. When it is seen, it's usually in a very close family where it has become a tradition to help provide the reception food for each bride as she comes along.

The family members decide, with the help of the bride, of course, who should bring what type of food, keeping the wedding theme in mind. If the reception has a Hawaiian luau theme, for example, the family may decide upon hollowed-out pineapples filled with fruit, Hawaiian breads, barbecued pork and roasted potato skins. There will usually be at least one talented aunt or grandma with the "gift of hospitality" who can come up with the menu. The family members prepare and store the food in their own homes until the day of the wedding.

Other than approving the menu, the bride and her family are relieved of any responsibilities other than the slight cost of $.73 per person to cover the paper products, if required, such as plates, utensils, napkins, cups and plastic tumblers.

Cake and Beverage Only
Cost . . . . $2.48/person, $744/300 guests

Paper products	$ .73
Coffee, tea and champagne punch	1.25
Mints	.20
Nuts	.30
Total	$2.48/person

(The cake, of course, is an additional cost.)

The Pro-Am Combo
Cost . . . . $3.06/person, $918/300 guests

Under this plan the main meat dishes are purchased from a professional source, such as a delicatessen, caterer or food service supplier. All the side dishes, such as salads, breads, condiments, vegetable trays, fruit trays or chips and dips, are donated by family and friends. When friends or relatives ask if there is anything they can do to help, have a list of ideas with you in your notebook at all times, and suggest a couple of side dishes for the reception. People are happy to help out if you're ready with suggestions. By the way, the menu that follows offers suggestions for your pro-am combo, but you may have even better ideas in mind. This menu will be helpful as a guideline for costs:

*Lasagne	$ .75
*Meatballs	.33
Paper products	.73
Coffee, punch and champagne punch	1.25
Total	$3.06/person

*Can be made and frozen ahead of time.

I found delicious lasagne and meatballs for sale at a wholesale food supplier, for example. The lasagne came in trays of sixteen servings for $11 and the meatballs were frozen in a huge plastic sack, 190 medium meatballs for about $15. I figured one serving of lasagne and three meatballs per person.

Amateur Hors d'Oeuvres
Cost. . . . . **$4.31/person, $1,293/300 guests**

*Meatballs on frill picks	$ .36
Fruit kabobs on mini-skewers	.39
*Petite quiche	.33
*Egg rolls	.48
Olives	.12
Pickles	.15
Mints	.20
Nuts	.30
Paper products	.73
Coffee, tea and champagne punch	1.25
Total	$4.31/person

*Can be made and frozen ahead of time.

The meatballs, fruit, petite quiche and egg rolls can be purchased from a wholesale food supplier. The fruit kabobs are made by sticking wooden skewers through fresh or frozen fruit pieces. They are then poked into a head of red cabbage which creates a colorful table display. Just be sure to flatten the bottom of the cabbage so it won't roll around.

Amateur Breakfast Buffet
Cost. . . . . **$4.44/person, $1,332/300 guests**

Scrambled eggs with ham bits	$ .54
*Biscuits	.40
*Cinnamon rolls	.39
*Potatoes O'Brien	.52
Baked apples	.27
Paper products	.73
Coffee, tea and champagne punch	1.59
Total	$4.44/person

*Can be made and frozen ahead of time.

The reason this breakfast menu is so reasonable is that the meat cost is kept to a minimum by merely sprinkling ham bits into the eggs. The biscuits and the cinnamon rolls can be purchased from the wholesale food service suppliers. The Potatoes

O'Brien come frozen in your supermarket. The apples need to be cored, sprinkled with cinnamon and sugar and baked upright for one hour at 325 degrees—delicious! Most reception venue kitchens have ovens to accommodate this number of apples; otherwise, they will need to be baked, twenty-five at a time, in the home ovens of friends and family members. It isn't necessary for the apples to be served hot out of the oven; just so they aren't served cold.

The orange juice can be made from concentrate or poured straight from the can. Just float a few orange slices and add a little champagne for sparkle!

This buffet is very tricky because the eggs and potatoes need to be prepared and served hot at the last minute. You'll need at least two volunteers to keep three skillets of scrambled eggs going all the time. Whip the eggs ahead of time so the cooks have nothing to do but "scramble." This breakfast buffet is guaranteed to please your guests without wiping out your life savings.

Amateur Luncheon Buffet
Cost. . . . . $5.13/person, $1,539/300 guests

Dolly roll sandwiches	$ .97
Fruit salad	.39
Potato salad	.32
Mixed bean salad	.35
Pickled beet salad	.35
Olives	.12
Pickles	.15
Nuts	.30
Mints	.20
Coffee, tea and champagne punch	1.25
Paper products	.73

Total $5.13/person

The fruit salad is sold by wholesale suppliers by the gallon. It can be poured into bowls for serving. The potato salad comes in ten-pound cartons. The mixed bean salad and pickled beets come in a can, already prepared. The Dolly sandwiches will receive rave reviews and are so easy to prepare that I'm almost embarrassed to give you this recipe.

For each 100 guests

One twenty-pound turkey

One gallon jar of mayonnaise

Chopped celery (one hundred short pieces, ready to chop, or approximately five pounds)

Salt and pepper to taste

Dolly rolls

The mayonnaise and celery chunks can be purchased from the wholesale supplier. The mayonnaise costs about $3.48 per gallon and the celery runs approximately $4. The Dolly rolls are available from a bakery at approximately $.21 each when purchased twenty-four at a time. They are the size of a tennis ball and make a filling and delectable sandwich. I've allowed two of these sandwiches per guest.

Bake the turkey in your oven, unstuffed, per directions. Strip all the meat off the turkey, both light and dark, and put it through a meat grinder. Add the mayo and chopped celery. The turkey can be baked, stripped and frozen months in advance. The mayo and celery can be added a day or two before the reception and refrigerated in large resealable bags. Then, during the reception itself, one or two volunteers place ''puffy scoops'' inside the Dolly rolls and serve the sandwiches fresh on buffet platters. By using a small ice cream scoop, the actual preparation goes very fast. In order to prevent spoilage, it's important to keep the turkey-mayo mixture cold until it's scooped onto the buns.

Amateur Dinner Buffet
Cost. . . . . $6.04/person, $1,812/300 guests

*Baked half-breasts of chicken	$ 1.29
*Parsley potatoes	.46
*Glazed whole red beets	.37
Fruit salad compote cups	.45
*Rolls	.21
Tomato slices	.30
*Butter chips	.21
Olives	.12
Pickles	.15
Nuts	.30
Mints	.20
Coffee, tea and champagne punch	1.25
Paper products	.73
Total	$6.04/person

*Can be made and frozen ahead of time.

Purchase all the products at your wholesale supplier. The half-breasts of chicken are approximately five ounces each and run about $1.29 each when bought in bulk. They can be baked a month or so in advance and frozen until the big day. The canned potatoes are prepared by merely heating in hot margarine and rolling in parsley flakes. They are easily prepared at the last minute.

The beets also come canned and need to be heated with a little brown sugar to form a glaze. The fruit salad is the same as on the luncheon buffet, except that it's mixed with a little instant pudding mix and served in small compote glasses for a dressier look. The ratio of pudding to fruit salad should be about 1.3 ounces of dry pudding mix to every 7 pounds of fruit salad. Vanilla instant pudding mix is merely dumped, dry from the box, into the fruit salad; the liquid in the fruit salad combines with the mix to give it a creamy thickness. The fruit doesn't need to be drained first because the liquid combines with the mix to cause the thickening process. The red tomato slices, as with the red beets and fruit salad, add color to the table.

Hire the Parish Crew
Cost. . . . . $12/person, $3,600/300 guests

Many churches provide a kitchen crew who will prepare and serve the reception food. Their menus vary as widely as their beliefs, so you will need to check them out. They serve everything from cold lunchmeat and salad buffets to full sit-down dinners. Some even offer ethnic dishes, such as Swedish Cabbage Rolls or Pepper-cocker Cookies. The $12 per person cost would probably include sliced luncheon meats, cheeses, rolls, mustard, mayonnaise, lettuce, tomato slices, olives, pickles, two types of salad (one pasta and one gelatin), mints, nuts, coffee, tea or punch.

The main advantage of this plan is that it includes all the annoying little extras, such as paper products, tables, linens, serving and cleanup.

Reception Advice

You *must* have someone in charge other than the bride, her mother or members of the wedding party. Preferably, you should have a supervisor and two to three helpers. The best candidates for these volunteer positions are friends or relatives of the bride who have sincerely offered to help in this regard. If you don't have a volunteer to fill this position, call the career placement office at your local college to hire a dependable college student; pay this student well! Even if you have to pay a supervisor $20 or $25 an hour for six hours of work, it will be worth it to you for the thousands of dollars you can save with these economical plans.

The supervisor will keep food on the table by alternating plates. This means that for every food item there is at least one tray on the buffet table and one in the kitchen being refilled. The minute a tray on the buffet table looks "picked at," it needs to be replaced by a fresh one. Then the sloppy one is taken to the kitchen to be added to and "fixed up" for the next replacement. The guests will think you have an endless supply of freshly prepared food. One of the helpers needs to be the "kitchen magician" who achieves this miracle.

The other helpers should roam among the guests offering any extra food as well as coffee, tea and punch.

You'll notice that I always include champagne punch, assuming that you're on a budget and can't afford the normal one-half bottle of champagne per person, which is what caterers suggest. Here is my very own "secret" wedding punch recipe:

For every 60 servings

Kool-Aid (Make the Kool-Aid ahead of time by mixing the powder with water according to directions on the can.)	$ 5.60
Sherbet, half gallon	3.00
Generic lemon-lime soda pop, two bottles (two liters each)	1.38
Champagne, one bottle (750 ml)	6.00
Total	$15.98

The punch can be made with raspberry Kool-Aid and raspberry sherbet, lime Kool-Aid and lime sherbet, or orange Kool-Aid and orange sherbet. Instead of using regular ice in the punch, which tends to water it down, make ice blocks ahead of time by freezing some of the Kool-Aid in large plastic cups. As you pour the soda pop and champagne onto the dollops of sherbet, the punch will foam and bubble and look *very* expensive. Everyone will want the recipe, but you can just "play dumb" if you don't want to divulge the ingredients! I played dumb for years, until now! You are the first to receive my "secret recipe." Of course, if you decide to skip the champagne, the cost will be even less. By the way, for that special added touch float orange, lemon or lime slices on top.

Creating a Beautiful Buffet Table

My last bit of advice pertains to the "presentation" of the buffet table. Any caterer or hotel chef will tell you that the most important factor is the way the food appears to the guests. When your guests enter the reception hall and see the food, you *must* hear "oooohs" and "aaahs," and here are the ways to get them:

1. Fill the table with color for eye appeal. In addition to the colors in the foods themselves, fill in between the dishes with flowers, greenery, ribbons, crepe paper streamers or pyramids of fresh fruit and candles. Close your eyes and try to picture the last time you enjoyed a Sunday brunch at a nice restaurant. Remember the color and interest tucked in and around the food trays?

2. "Mirror" the dishes—that is, have two of every dish, one at each end of the table. This will make it look like "more."

Buffet Table Layout

☙ *Raised tray of finger foods*

Just as important as how the food tastes is how the food looks. An effective buffet presentation will impress your guests and help create an atmosphere of opulence, even on a budget.

3. Elevate the food dishes. *NEVER, NEVER, NEVER* serve trays flat on the table! The difference between your buffet table and a church potluck is the presentation of your food. Place the food on cigar boxes filled with bricks and covered with white linen napkins or a "staircase" made out of heavy books covered with a tablecloth. Go crazy with your imagination! Pretend you are a great chef who is being judged on creativity!

4. Garnish the food trays themselves. You don't need to spend hours carving wedding bells out of radishes or love birds out of apples, but you must add something! Here are some ideas:

- "Frame" each dish with green leaf lettuce

- Add parsley

- Add huge, fresh strawberries

- Add melon slices, especially bright red watermelon

- Add fresh pineapple chunks

- Add fresh flowers

I know you'll do an amazing job—I wish I could be there to see it!

Create Interesting and Enticing Food Stations

Food stations are the latest trend in reception food service (as opposed to traditional buffet tables). Each food station is a separate smaller table that serves a certain type of food, such as seafood, prime rib (where a chef stands carving), hors d'oeuvres, fruit and cheese, finger sandwiches, chip and dip, desserts, and so forth. The reasons why these stations are so trendy are because: they make simple foods seem like "more"; the guests enjoy moving around the room, visiting with other guests who are clustered around the various stations; and many guests can be served at the same time. One bride I know decided to have a dessert reception, and spread food stations around the garden, each with its own specialty dessert. She had a "Chocolate Station," "Sundae and Frozen Yogurt Station," "Pie Station," and a "Custom Crepe Station." By offering all these desserts, she only needed a small wedding cake.

Of course, in addition to your food stations, you'll always need a beverage table and a cake table.

Coffee and punch may be served from the same beverage table or each can have its own table. Quantities vary widely depending on time of day, time of year, type of food, whether it's hot outside or cold. On a warm or hot day when there is icy cold punch, you may not need more than 40–50 cups of coffee. If you have two percolators available, you can always get the second one going while filling your coffee urns from the other, ensuring there is always enough on hand. By the way, cappuccino and espresso drinks are becoming popular alternatives to alcoholic beverages.

The Wedding Cake

The wedding cake is almost as much fun to shop for as the wedding gown! I had admired the wedding cakes displayed in bakeries for years, wondering when our daughter would find the right guy. Then the time came—we actually walked into a bakery to price a cake for her real-live wedding! We ordered a four-layer cake that, along with extra sheet cakes served out of the kitchen, would serve at least 250 people. We could easily have done without the side cakes because only about half the guests wanted dessert. Evidently, this is almost always the case, so don't feel you must provide one serving of cake per guest.

If you haven't priced a wedding cake lately, they're averaging about $3 per slice, or $600 for two hundred servings. That's the bad news. Now for the money-saving magic. The following ideas will help you cut costs dramatically.

Dummy Cake + Donated Sheet Cakes
Approximate Cost $90

Assemble a "dummy cake" made out of Styrofoam. Have it frosted by an amateur who makes wedding cakes out of her home. Most amateurs I spoke with said they would charge approximately $50 to frost a dummy cake. Decorate it with your own cake topper or fresh flowers from the supermarket. If you fill the top of each layer with fresh flowers, you can usually get away with frosting the sides yourself. The combination of amateur frosting, supermarket flowers and inexpensive cake top will total about $70; including the cost of the Styrofoam layers, the entire cake will cost about $90. The "dummy cake layers" (actually, rounds of Styrofoam) can be purchased at craft and wedding supply stores, or if you can't find them pre-cut in rounds, purchase rectangular pieces, two-inches thick, which can be cut into rounds using a serrated knife. Rub the sides of the rounds against each other to smooth off any rough spots. Here are typical prices for two-inch thick "layers":

6″ round	$ 2.50
8″ round	4.00
10″ round	5.00
12″ round	5.50
14″ round	12.90
18″ round	19.50

* These costs will be much less if you cut your own rounds out of standard rectangular sheets of Styrofoam, which are available in almost all craft stores.

By the way, as long as it's a "fake cake" anyway, you might as well make a big one. Then trail ribbons or cascade more flowers from layer to layer. Of course, you'll need to provide one small decorated cake that will sit in back of the large "dummy cake" for the bride and groom to cut during the reception, or you can insert a wedge of real cake into the bottom layer of Styrofoam, frosted over in such a way that only the bride and groom know it's there. Your guests will be amazed! What they won't know is that they're actually being fed donated sheet cakes out of the kitchen, sliced onto little cake plates and served on trays. These sheet cakes will be donated by all those wonderful friends and relatives who ask "if there is anything at all they can do to help." You'll need twelve to fifteen sheet cakes cut to feed twenty guests each, and they should be the same type of cake—white with white icing, or chocolate with white icing, and so forth.

> *Tip* You may want to bake a small cake to be used as the top layer of the dummy cake, instead of using Styrofoam. That way you'll have it to save and freeze until your first wedding anniversary when you can pull it out and enjoy it with your friends and family.

Dummy Cake + Bake Your Own Sheet Cakes
Approximate Cost *$135*

Under this plan you add to the $90 dummy cake sheet cakes that you baked yourself. The cost of the packaged cake mix, oil and eggs for fifteen sheet cakes will be approximately $45. Bake these cakes ahead and freeze them—a really painless process. You'll have cakes stored in "volunteer freezers" all over town, but it's worth the trouble.

Buy From a Private Party
Approximate Cost *$200*

There are some wonderful cooks out there who make wedding cakes for a living. We have several in our town. One good way to find these jewels is by word-of-mouth; talk to anyone you know who has planned a wedding recently, talk to your club and church friends and, best of all, keep an eye out for cake decorating classes being offered by your local crafts store or community college. These instructors may bake and decorate wedding cakes as a little side business or, if not, they may know of someone who does. In any case, be *sure* to get references.

Buy a Supermarket Cake
Approximate Cost *$175*

You'll be pleasantly surprised at supermarket bakery prices, which average about $1.40 per serving. I can hardly believe it myself, and I've seen these cakes with my very own eyes. How they can make such a large, beautifully decorated cake for such a low price is beyond me, but definitely worth your consideration. When I checked out supermarket cakes for my last revision of this book, the prices were great, but the selections were poor—most of the supermarket bakeries only offered white cake with white frosting. Things have changed, however, and today's supermarket wedding cakes come with many options, as you'll see below.

The cake tops are extra, but you can save money there by opting for one of the affordable cake top ideas given at the end of this chapter.

As this book goes to print, here are just a few of the wedding cakes available through supermarket bakeries in my hometown of Tucson, Arizona:

❦ "Enchanted Pearls" (2 tier) 80 servings $99.99

❦ "Enchanted Pearls" (3 tier) 106 servings $149.99

❦ "Waves of Passion" (2 tier) 80 servings $99.99

❦ "Waves of Passion" (3 tier) 106 servings $149.99

❦ "White Renaissance" (2 tier) 80 servings $99.99

❦ "White Renaissance" (3 tier) 106 servings $149.99

❦ "Dotted Swiss" (2 tier) 80 servings $89.99

❦ "Dotted Swiss" (3 tier) 106 servings $139.99

❦ "Staircase of Dreams" (7 tier) 206 servings $349.99

❦ "White Orchid" (4 tier) 130 servings $199.99

❦ "Garden Romance" (3 tier) 106 servings $159.99

❦ "Death by Chocolate" (Groom's Cake) 48 servings $39.99

❦ Wedding Sheet Cake 24 servings $19.99

❦ Cake Flavors
White, Marble, Chocolate and Carrot

❦ Filling Flavors
Lemon, Cherry, Strawberry, Vanilla and Pineapple

❦ Frosting Flavors
Vanilla Buttercreme, Chocolate Buttercreme, White Whipped Topping, Chocolate Whipped Topping or Cream Cheese

These cakes are exquisite, provided with clear crystal columns. The seven-tier "Staircase of Dreams" is really a showpiece with three tiers perched above a crystal fountain, plus two smaller cakes on each side of the central tiers, connected by bridges.

The reason I've provided so much detail on these particular supermarket bakery cakes is so you'll know how affordable and elegant supermarket wedding cakes have become.

Smaller Wedding Cake + Side Cakes
Approximate Cost *$250*

Order a small wedding cake and a few sheet cakes from a professional bakery.

Affordable Cake Toppers

In addition to the simple idea of adding fresh flowers to your wedding cake, here are some other affordable cake topper ideas:

❦ **Wine Glass With Flowers**
Stand a wine glass on a round mirror for stability; fill it with silk flowers and tufted netting; tie the stem of the glass with a bow and add swirls of tulle netting around the edge of the mirror.

❦ **Tiny White Basket With Flowers**
Use this same idea, only with a basket instead of a wine glass.

❦ **Framed Photo of the Bride and Groom**
The trick to this simple cake topper is to round up an elegant white ceramic or lacy crystal frame for the couple's photo; set it on a five-inch by one-inch base of white Styrofoam covered with silk flowers, tufts of white tulle netting and strings of white seed pearls, one of which drapes over an upper corner of the frame.

❦ **Bride and Groom Figurines**
Surely you know someone who collects Precious Moments figurines; ask if you can borrow one of a bride and groom, setting the bisque figurine on a mirror with sprigs of white silk stephanotis sprinkled around the edge of the mirror and at the feet of the bride and groom.

❦ **Blown Glass**
There are dozens of traditional blown glass figures that work just as well, from two hearts entwined, to a wishing well, to a pair of love doves, to a wedding bell suspended from a heart.

❦ *Wired Ribbon Bows*

I saw a wedding cake recently that was beautifully adorned with affordable wired ribbon bows. The top layer had a large three-inch wired bow "sitting up" on top. The remaining layers each had five smaller one and one-half inch wired bows placed evenly around each layer. Each of the bows had their "tails" draping gracefully down onto the next layer by about two inches. The bows were in the primary wedding color—a soft, dusty pink. What a simple, affordable, yet elegant way to decorate a white wedding cake.

❦ *"Nested" Votive Candles*

I recently discovered another clever, affordable, yet stunning, way to top a wedding cake. The theme of the wedding was white, in varying shades, plus hundreds of candles, some tall and tapered, some short and fat, others floating in clear crystal bowls. So, in keeping with the theme, the entire wedding cake was also aglow with candles. The white frosted cake was arranged in single stair step layers, each with several white nested votive candles. By "nested" I mean that the shallow votive candles were pressed down into the frosting so that the sides of the candles were hidden from view. This was an evening wedding and when the lights were dimmed and all the candles were lit, including those on the cake, the reception venue evolved into a magical setting, all because of flaming romantic candlelight.

❦ *Rotating Music Box*

Borrow a music box that complements your theme; set it on a mirror, surround the base with silk flowers and narrow acetate ribbons and then appoint someone to be in charge of winding the music box off and on during the reception. It will be a real conversation piece!

If you're interested in a few more ideas, including some that require a little bit more time and "crafting ability," such as customized cake toppers to complement your reception theme, you may want to pick up a copy of my book entitled *Beautiful Wedding Decorations & Gifts on a Small Budget*.

Tip Not only has it become fashionable to borrow your mother's or grandmother's wedding gown or veil, it is also trendy to borrow their wedding cake top, especially if it has been well preserved through the years. This will add a meaningful, nostalgic quality to your wedding cake.

Other Food Expenses

Besides the reception food, which is the biggest expense of all, there are other "feedings," as well. The following ideas will help you pull everything together with grace and style.

The Bridesmaids' Luncheon

The bridesmaids' luncheon is traditionally held the Saturday before the wedding. There is often an exchange of gifts during this luncheon. The bridesmaids may give the bride a joint gift and the bride will probably give each of her attendants something personal—usually jewelry that can be worn during the wedding.

It's common for the cost of this luncheon to be shared "Dutch treat" by all in attendance, although it may be paid entirely by either the bride or bridesmaids. This little luncheon can be held in a restaurant or a home. It's the duty of the maid or matron of honor to be sure this luncheon date is set.

The Rehearsal Dinner

Lucky for the bride's family—the rehearsal dinner is the responsibility of the groom's family. It's become quite acceptable, however, for those on both sides of the family to "pitch in" and help with this dinner. It can be a spaghetti dinner, an old-fashioned picnic or a barbecue in someone's backyard. Things can get silly after the wedding rehearsal, so there's no need for a formal sit-down dinner; although a member of either family may welcome the opportunity to entertain the wedding party with a sit-down dinner in their home dining room. Another good idea is to go "Dutch treat" to a local restaurant where a private room has been reserved. Of course, if the groom's family wishes to have the dinner catered, that's great, too.

Pre-Wedding Snacks

You'll need to provide some kind of nourishment for the nervous wedding party, especially for those who arrive early to dress at the church or synagogue.

If it's a morning wedding, you may want to provide a continental breakfast of coffee, juice and rolls. If the wedding is later in the day, small finger sandwiches are good, as well as cookies and fruit. Just be sure they aren't drippy or messy. This snack should be light, easy and inexpensive. Make things to freeze ahead if you can.

Feed the Musicians, Photographer and Videographer

You'll need to provide some kind of nourishment for these contracted workers, although nothing as elaborate or expensive as the fare you're serving your guests. Usually, a simple hot plate or a tray of sandwiches and chips is fine. Provide a separate setting for these workers to take their refreshment.

Feed Those Houseguests!

If ever you don't feel like having houseguests, it's when you're hosting a wedding, but they come anyway, complete with their party spirit, bubbly enthusiasm and hearty appetites. The best advice I can give you is to go to your friendly wholesale food supplier and buy trays of lasagne. Remember them from the ''Pro-Am Combo'' plan? You can feed a lot of houseguests for the money, just add a salad, rolls and a light dessert.

I hope this chapter has given you some good ideas. Now, we're ready to tackle the music.

7

And-A-One-And-A-Two . . .

(Affordable Melodies)

Imagine a wedding ceremony and reception without music! How flat! How boring! It would be about as exciting as a nap.

Music is the glue that holds all the pieces together—the flowers and the flounce, the ribbons and the rice, the dress and the "I dos." The strains of the violin or the strum of the guitar—these are the subtle wooings that bring a tear to the eye and a lump to the throat. You may be counting on an organ that shakes the pillars as the bride walks down the aisle on the arm of her dad; and you must have a reception hall that shouts with the same joy being felt by all. But, how will you afford it? And what does it cost, anyway?

If you were one of those writing "a check a day," you would merely arrange for union vocalists at $150 each, a harpist at $175 per hour and an organist at $110. Then you would hire two ten-piece bands to play during the reception—one with music for the younger generation and one with the classics for the older folks. During the bands' breaks your strolling guitarists would entertain the guests as they nibble on their caviar.

You, however, are on a different kind of budget. Even if you could hire a smaller band, a professional four-piece group for four hours would cost you from $600 to $1,500. Or you might consider a "Mobile Disc Jockey Music Service," also known as a "DJ." This clever person, with complete mixer setup, microphone and customized sound system, will cost you between $250 and $1,200 for four hours.

All of these fees vary, of course, according to the part of the country where you live, with higher costs in the large metropolitan areas, lower costs in the midwest, and so forth.

There are some clever ways around these expenses, however. Here are some of the most popular:

Cutting the Cost of Ceremony Music
Free Recital
No Cost *$0*

Under this plan your musically talented friends and relatives donate all the music, both vocally and instrumentally. You probably have much more talent in your family and circle of acquaintances than you even realize. Ask around and you may find that your niece plays the harp beautifully in her school orchestra, or that your cousin is an accomplished flautist. A word of caution: the music is one of the most important contributions to the mood of your day and you certainly don't want a shaky performance, so you may want to stage a discreet audition. In any case, ask for recommendations from others who have heard the performances.

Pro-Am Combo
Approximate Cost *$75*

Hire one professional, such as the church organist, and fill in the rest with "free recital" talent. An excellent organist is sometimes the most difficult to find and you may have to pay for one's services. Nothing is more disconcerting than a novice who makes the church organ sound like a carnival calliope, but by hiring the church organist you'll pay much less than a union musician provided by a professional agency.

On the other hand, you may have an accomplished organist in the family, but not a single person who can sing in public without trembling. In this case, use the free organist and splurge on a local vocalist who sings at weddings for a "nonprofessional" fee. You can find these talented people by talking to recent brides or to the head of the Music Department of your local university, who will be happy to recommend outstanding music students who not only need the experience, but the extra money as well. After all, even a "Big Mac," fries and a Coke dig into a student's meager budget.

Canned and Fresh
Approximate Cost *$75*

Use "canned music," via cassette tape or a CD, combined with a real live $75 vocalist who will sing to a taped accompaniment. The cassette tape or CD will have prerecorded music that you have selected. The music will be in the order of the ceremony, beginning with the seating of the guests and ending with the recessional. Your public library has tapes and CDs of suitable music. Check them out and record your favorite selections onto your ceremony tape. Be sure the library's copy is in excellent condition with no scratches or skips. If necessary, invest in a new copy of the album to assure high quality. When recording onto your ceremony tape, use very high fidelity recording equipment. You certainly don't want the wedding march to sound muddy or tinny. If your own recording equipment is inferior for this purpose, find an audiophile friend who will make this recording for you on high-quality, state-of-the-art equipment.

This plan obviously requires a volunteer to start and stop the tape which, preferably, will be played over the church's sound system.

All Local Talent
> *Approximate Cost* *$150*

Hire three non-union musicians at $50 each. In addition to an organist, you'll probably need one vocalist and one other instrumentalist. These nonprofessional people are available locally and frequently perform at weddings. You may discover them when you hear them perform at a church or another wedding. Ask for suggestions from church staffs and recent brides and, again, check with the university music department.

Cutting the Cost of Reception Music
Free Recital
> *No Cost* *$0*

Just as with the ceremony, the "Free Recital" musicians are your talented relatives and friends. You'll find that musicians for your reception will be easier to find than for the ceremony, mainly because the reception music is usually less formal. Sniff around for a talented local band, guitarist or pianist.

Piped-In Music
> *No Cost* *$0*

This idea is too good to be true—free music available over the sound system. Many halls have background music that is already programmed and ready to use. Ask when you reserve your reception site. There are so many wonderful tracks available these days, but if the music is the "elevator" variety, you won't be interested. Be sure to listen to it ahead of time.

Amateur DJ
> *No Cost* *$0*

A professional DJ would run anywhere from $250 to $1,200, depending on whether it's a Saturday evening reception and what part of the country you live in. An "Amateur DJ" will provide the service for free, or for a small honorarium. Where do you find these jewels? You may have a talented teenager available within your own family; otherwise, ask friends and recent brides for recommendations. You'll need a guy or gal with two qualities: the ability to speak clearly into a microphone, thus doubling as your Master of Ceremonies, plus the ability to take direction, especially when it comes to dress, volume and choice of music.

You'll also need help rounding up the musical selections you want played, but between the music the DJ has available, plus music you already have available at home or through your local library, you'll come up with plenty to fill the time. The library is an especially good source for ethnic and specialty music, such as the hora, polka or the tango.

Party Tapes
No Cost *$0*

This plan is similar to the last one, except that the music is provided on a series of one-hour cassette tapes that have been pre-recorded with your own selection of music. Take time in the weeks before the wedding to transfer music from CDs and tapes (including ethnic and specialty numbers) onto the reception tapes. Number them in order and have someone responsible to play them in order on cue. For example, Tape No. 1 might have music suitable for the beginning of the reception, during the receiving line. Tape No. 2 might begin with the bride and groom's first dance, followed by the rest of the dance music. Tape No. 3 may have music appropriate during the food service, cake cutting, and so forth.

Two-for-One Sale
Approximate Cost **$100**

Hire the same person to be the organist at the ceremony and the pianist at the reception. It's less expensive to hire one person to perform at both functions than to hire two separate musicians. Most organists also play the piano very well, but this is only a suggestion—you may know an organist who is talented on a number of other instruments, giving you a choice.

All Local Talent
Approximate Cost **$250**

In lieu of a professional band, which can run from $750 to $5,000, depending on your part of the country, why not hire a small band composed of local students or a string trio or brass quartet. Keep your eyes and ears open when you attend other functions. The talent is out there and you can find it.

❧

The music for our daughter's wedding cost $185. We had three musicians at $40 each, including the church pianist and organist, a vocalist who accompanied herself on the guitar at $40 and two soloists, one of whom donated her services. The other charged $25.

The ceremony music was classical with a flute/harpsichord duet, piano and organ music, a vocal solo and a vocal duet. The only reception music that we paid for was the tearjerker, "Sunrise, Sunset," from *Fiddler on the Roof,* sung by a wonderful soprano who accompanied herself on the guitar. She sang the song to accompany a touching slide presentation showing the bride and groom from babyhood to engagement. There weren't too many dry eyes!

Musical Advice

Because you are serving as your own wedding consultant, these are some things you should know about planning the music:

1. Always check with the clergyman or rabbi before planning the ceremony music. There are various rules you may need to follow. Some religious denominations, for example, don't approve of the traditional wedding march. Others will not allow any secular music at all. You'll also need permission to use the sound system.

2. Ask a church organist for musical ideas for the ceremony.

3. Be careful that you don't use music as a "filler" or mere entertainment during the ceremony. The ceremony music should be selected because of its solemnity.

4. Familiarize yourself with the traditional music usually played or sung during a wedding ceremony. This will help you make your selections, even if you do deviate from the norm. Our daughter, for instance, chose the "Wedding March" from *The Sound of Music* for her recessional, which was played by the church organist.

For the very latest trends in ceremony and reception music, visit these Web sites:

www.weddingtips.com/wtfavori.html

www.ultimatewedding.com/songs/

Meanwhile, as this book goes to print, here are some popular favorites for you to consider:

Prelude selections:

"Arioso" by Bach

"Canon in D" by Pachebel

"Air from Water Music" by Handel

"Moonlight Sonata" by Beethoven

"Clair de Lune" by Debussy

"Trumpet Tune" by Purcell

"Larghetto" by Handel

"Adagio" by Liszt

Three favorite processionals are:

"Aria in F Major" by Handel

"March in C" by Purcell

"Trumpet Voluntary" by Jeremiah Clarke

Here are some of the traditional love songs sung during the ceremony:

"The Greatest of These Is Love" by Bitgood

"O Perfect Love" by Barnby

"I Love Thee" by Grieg

If you decide to break the classical tradition, here are more modern love songs:

"Follow Me" by John Denver

"We've Only Just Begun" by Roger Nichols

"Hawaiian Wedding Song" by Al Hoffman and Dick Manning

"All I Ask of You" from *The Phantom of the Opera* by Webber, Hart and Stiltoe

"Evergreen" by Streisand and Williams

"Wedding Song" by Paul Stookey

"Do You Remember?" by J. Ivanovici

"Morning Has Broken" by Eleanor Farjeon

"What I Did for Love" by Marvin Hamlisch

Recessional selections:

"Joyful, Joyful, We Adore Thee" by Beethoven

"Hornpipe Water Music" by Handel

"Third Movement from Brandenburg Concerto #3" by Bach

"Toccata from Organ Symphony #5" by Widor

Anything goes at the reception, but here are some of the most popular "first dances" for the bride and groom:

"At Last" by Etta James

"Unforgettable" by Irving Gordon

"Wonderful Tonight" by Eric Clapton

"Grow Old Along With Me" by John Lennon

"Can You Feel the Love Tonight?" by John and Rice

"Just the Way You Are" by Billy Joel

"Could I Have This Dance" by Anne Murray

"Stand by Me" by Ben E. King

"I'll Always Love You" by Taylor Dane

Here are some of the most popular father-daughter and mother-son dance selections. For the father-daughter dance:

"Wind Beneath My Wings" by Silbar and Henley

"Just the Way You Are" by Billy Joel

"Sunrise, Sunset" from *Fiddler on the Roof* by Harnick and Bock

"Thank Heaven for Little Girls" from *Gigi* by Lerner and Loewe

"My Girl" by Robinson and White

"The Times of Your Life" by Paul Anka

For the mother-son dance

"You Are the Sunshine of My Life" by Stevie Wonder

"Wind Beneath My Wings" by Silbar and Henley

"Child of Mine" by Carole King

"My Mother's Eyes" by Gilbert and Baer

All these musical suggestions are given to inspire you to research for yourself. Go to your local music store and thumb through some wedding songbooks—you'll have no difficulty narrowing your choice to those precious selections that will give your day special beauty and meaning. Just beware of one thing: if you decide to use "Sunrise, Sunset," add a case of Kleenex to your shopping list!

❦   ❦   ❦

8

Clever, Cute and Crafty

(Ambience on a Budget)

The decorations require a creative spirit, an uninhibited imagination and a wide open mind. Following your theme, the decorations will establish a certain "feeling" or ambience for the ceremony and reception. The theme should be determined by two things: the formality of the wedding and the availability of decorative items and props you can borrow, rent, purchase, or make inexpensively.

If you were one of the "check-a-day" people, you wouldn't be concerned about cost because money can buy ambience. However, you're on a small budget, so you'll need an extra special "thinking cap" in order to come up with ideas that are "creative" and "cheap" at the same time—and that can make your brain hurt! Are you ready to take on the challenge? Great! Here's the signal—"Go for it!"

First of all, let's clarify what I mean by *ambience.* You'll have a better picture of the meaning after you hear descriptions of two recent weddings. The mood, or ambience, was very different in each case.

The first wedding was held in the evening two days after Christmas. The theme was a "Magical Forest" created by the use of a darkened sanctuary and reception hall, dozens of evergreen trees, tiny white lights and candles. When the usher seated me for the ceremony, there was a hush over the congregation as we sat in the semidarkness. Once our eyes adjusted, we realized that the sanctuary was filled with evergreen trees and boughs, all dressed in tiny white lights. Even the platform was loaded with lighted trees, plus candles that glowed on tall candelabras.

A talented classical pianist played softly—the piano was the only musical instrument used throughout the ceremony. The concept was really very simple, and yet it set an elegant and sanctified mood. When the bride came down the aisle to the strains of more classical music, she looked like the "dream princess" of her magical forest. She wore a sophisticated satin gown accented with silver sequins that reflected the subtle lights. No one dared breathe; it was as if we were characters in a fairy tale.

The same ambience prevailed at the reception. Even the long walkway that connected the sanctuary and reception site was dark except for light that spilled from the evergreen trees that lined it. As we walked from the sanctuary to the reception, we spoke in whispers. We squinted as we entered the reception hall, which was decorated with more evergreen trees and their twinkling white lights. There were several small round tables scattered around the room, each with a single white candle centerpiece. A different type of hors d'oeuvre was served at each table. The pianist was already at the grand piano and the same quiet classical music continued. Again, we spoke very softly and when I left the reception, I felt like I was giving up a magical dream and returning to the real world.

Even though the mood for this wedding and reception was one of royal elegance, it had been very simply created by the use of leftover trees that had practically been given away by frustrated Christmas tree vendors (the wedding was two days after Christmas, remember), candles bought by the gross, and borrowed Christmas tree lights. And, look at the result—a wonderful example of an expensive-looking ambience on a tight budget!

The second wedding had an opposite mood. It was a happy, loud, colorful, daytime wedding with a frolicking, festive reception. The sanctuary was decorated with several dozen grapevine wreaths, including two enormous ones that hung in back of the platform. They were wrapped with ribbons and dotted with bright flowers and natural greenery from a "free florist." The candles and pew boughs were bright lavender and peach. The organ was as tastefully loud and lively as were the bridesmaids' dresses. I would call the sanctuary theme "Happy Springtime!"

The reception was a grand party with a circus theme, including a circus master who served as master of ceremonies. There were clowns, a balloon sculptor and a mime. The wedding colors were repeated with the use of crepe paper, balloons and a "big top" made from plain brown butcher paper suspended from the ceiling.

The guests were animated and good-humored, all because of the deliberate use of inexpensive props and decorations that created the festive atmosphere. The bride and her sister made all the grapevine wreaths for the sanctuary, starting from scratch with actual grapevines from the San Joaquin Valley in California. The reception theme evolved from the availability of friends who agreed to perform as circus master, mime and balloon sculptor. Meanwhile, the crepe paper, balloons (nonhelium variety) and tent top were very affordable.

The contrasting settings of these two weddings demonstrate the importance of a theme. The first wedding and reception had a formal, classical theme, while the second deviated from tradition with its light-hearted party atmosphere. The important thing to remember is that, subtle or in-your-face, you *must have some kind of theme*. The theme is the skeleton that will support your plans; it affects every decision you'll make, from the wedding colors to the length of the gowns and from the melodies to the cake top. Choose your theme carefully; it should not be used as a gimmick, but as a true reflection of the personalities of the bride and groom.

Ethnic Themes

If you have an ethnic background, take advantage of it when planning your wedding, even if the traditions haven't been passed down in your family. What proud and wonderful traditions you have—rekindle as many as possible by incorporating them into your ceremony and reception.

Here are just a few ethnic wedding traditions that may inspire you to plan your entire wedding around your ethnic background.

Mexican

The Mexican bride and groom are bound together during the ceremony with a white cord, symbolizing their union.

During the couple's first dance, the guests form a heart-shaped ring around the couple.

German

The bride carries salted bread in her pocket, which is said to ensure bounty; the groom carries grain, ensuring wealth and good fortune.

Chinese

The bride and groom drink wine from goblets that have been tied together with a red ribbon or string (red symbolizes love and joy in China).

Egyptian

The bride's right wrist is tied to the groom's left wrist during the ceremony or the reception (a.k.a. "Tying the Knot").

Puerto Rican

A doll is placed in the center of the bride and groom's table at the wedding reception.

Greek

During the wedding ceremony, a Greek couple is connected by matching crowns, often made from orange blossoms, a symbol of fertility.

A Greek bride tucks ivy into her wedding bouquet, symbolizing her endless love for her groom.

While the couple is dancing during the wedding reception, guests approach the bride, one by one, and pin money to her gown.

Finnish

During the ceremony a Finnish bride wears a crown; after the ceremony, she holds her crown in her hands as she is blindfolded and girls dance around her in a circle.

She places the crown on the head of one of the dancing girls, who is said to be the next to marry.

Jewish

The Jewish bridegroom breaks a glass at the end of the wedding ceremony to call to mind the incompleteness of all rejoicing as long as the temple in Jerusalem remains in ruins.

French

After the wedding ceremony, the bride and groom drink a wedding toast from a single two-handled cup.

African-American

The bride and groom jump over a broom immediately following their wedding ceremony, symbolizing their love and commitment to each other as they establish their new home together.

Polish

The bride's friends weave a beautiful, intricate crown of rosemary leaves, which the bride wears during the wedding dance.

East Indian

On the wedding day, the groom's close friends and family members rub turmeric paste into his face and chest, which leaves his skin with a golden glow which is said to ward off bad spirits.

Japanese

As soon as the bride and groom exchange their wedding vows, the groom's brother, usually the best man, drops flower petals over the couple's heads.

Following the ceremony, the bride and groom take nine sips of sake; tradition says they become husband and wife after the first sip.

Korean

Guests at a Korean wedding reception (a.k.a. the "Noodle Banquet") are served noodle soup, consisting of beef broth, vegetables and long noodles (symbolizing a long and happy life for the couple).

English

The guests place a live or imitation spider on the bride's gown, which is said to bring good luck to the bride on her wedding day.

Danish

The Danes have a tradition during the wedding reception where the groom leaves the room so every man may kiss his bride, followed by the bride leaving the room so the women may kiss her groom.

Italian

During the wedding reception, the groom's tie is cut into small pieces which the groom sells to the guests to earn money for the honeymoon.

Research your own ethnic heritage for interesting traditions to be included in your wedding.

Traditional Themes

If you prefer the comfort of adopting a traditional theme, there are many choices to consider. It's interesting that traditional themes often include affordable garden-type settings that take advantage of cut flowers, flowering shrubs and other greenery provided from the gardens of friends and family members.

A Rose Garden

Fill the reception hall with as many roses as you can round up. Borrow potted and cut roses from friends and relatives. What you lack, buy in silks from your Oriental import outlet or favorite craft store. Be sure to buy them in sprays, as opposed to individual stems, which will give you more roses for the money. Cover the pots with paper in the wedding colors and tie with ribbons.

When you've borrowed or bought all the roses you can afford, fill the rest of the room with any other greenery you can find, including potted shrubs, trees or garlands made from natural greenery from the "free florist."

Once you've created a garden setting, set wrought iron or old-fashioned park benches among the greenery. Finish off the look with borrowed birdbaths. Stand pots of flowers in the birdbaths, or fill them with water and float rose petals or candles on top.

Hearts and Flowers

Use borrowed greenery of all kinds, dotted with flowers. The flowers can be any variety, but they should be wrapped with paper and ribbons in the wedding colors.

Cut hearts out of posterboard. The hearts should be in two sizes—six-inch and three-inch—and they should be in the primary wedding color. Use ribbons to hang them from the borrowed greenery; scatter them among the colorful flowers.

Use flowers as filler on the buffet table and place helium-filled heart-shaped balloons all over the hall. Tie them on the backs of chairs; tape them to the sides of the cake table.

Summer in the Park

We're back to a garden-type setting; this time the emphasis is on the wrought iron benches, birdbaths and the addition of old street lamps. If you can borrow only one of these decorative lamps, it will help set the mood.

Use the greenery ideas from "A Rose Garden" theme and the mixed flower ideas from the "Hearts and Flowers" theme. Add a "flower cart," whether real or pretend. It can be filled with flowers and trailed with ribbons.

Is this giving you some ideas? Here are some other traditional themes:

Paris in Springtime	Romantic Candlelight
Cupid and Love Doves	Autumn Harvest
Victorian Tea Party	Christmas Joy
Ice Palace	Valentine's Day
Winter Wonderland	

The ceremony themes (see page 102) may also carry over to the reception, which will save you a lot of work because you're only working with one theme, instead of two.

Nontraditional Themes

The latest trend in nontraditional themes is a costume wedding, such as Henry VIII English Tudor; Renaissance; Medieval; Folk; Halloween; Masked Ball; Western; Polynesian; Guys 'n Dolls; Romeo & Juliet; Elizabethan; Victorian; Edwardian; Greco-Roman; Southern Antebellum; Celtic; or any ethnic theme. Costumes for these weddings may be sewn from patterns, rented from costume shops, borrowed from theatrical production companies, rented or purchased through catalogs available at many bridal salons.

Here are some of the most popular nontraditional wedding themes:

Halloween Theme

Most Halloween weddings take place on Halloween itself. You have several choices when it comes to decor: "Spooky and Scary," "Autumn Harvest," "Elegant Candlelight Halloween" or "Mardi Gras." The Mardi Gras idea is especially popular because it lends itself to a masked ball where the guests try to guess each others' identities. Whatever your choice, be sure the wedding invitations ask the guests to arrive in costume. One of these weddings usually takes place in the evening for obvious reasons: you want the jack-o'-lanterns to glow, the candles to glimmer and the shadows to cast mysterious shapes around the venue. Instead of the traditional "scary face" jack-o'-lanterns, carve the bride's and groom's initials on the pumpkins face instead. Rather than the harsh black and orange usually seen at Halloween parties, you can gentle the color-scheme with a softer burnt orange and varied shades of gray. Decorate the tables with miniature pumpkins, tall tapered candles, half-masks and party streamers. Suspend black and orange balloons from the ceiling. If you choose the

Mardi Gras theme, you can give the guests traditional Mardi Gras beads to wear during the reception; if you go with a more traditional Halloween theme, give each guest a small "Trick or Treat" sack filled with candy corn, Hershey's kisses and a thank-you note from the bride and groom, written with black ink on orange paper.

Southern Antebellum Theme

A Southern antebellum theme lends itself to an outdoor venue, a mansion or any historical plantation type setting. Decorate with silk magnolia blossoms, gazebos, trellises, white picket fences and "parasols" (old umbrellas covered with crepe paper). Drape strings of small white lights around the wedding venue and place potted baby's breath on each reception table, along with Mason jars with lighted candles. The bride, her attendants and the reception hostesses may wear Southern belle gowns with hooped petticoats and carry armloads of hydrangeas, tulips or lilacs, tied at the stems with silk ribbons. The men may wear black trousers and white dinner jackets with pin-striped vests and ties. The bride and groom "getaway" in a horse and carriage.

Renaissance Theme

The Renaissance period began in the 1400s in Italy, then swept through the continent of Europe during the following two centuries. One of these weddings requires an outdoor setting, preferably near an old covered bridge, on a country farm or, if you're lucky, at a real-life historical castle. Renaissance brides often opt for a traditional ball gown of the era with bell-shaped sleeves, a V-shaped back and a bodice adorned with tiny pearls. The bride's attendants may wear flowing gowns and pointy hats and the men may wear velvet doublets, shirts with billowing sleeves and feathered hats. The groom may also wear a sword at his side. The wedding invitations should request, but not require, the guests to wear Renaissance attire. Musical entertainment may be provided by musicians playing a harp, guitar or a lute. The guests' favors may be burlap bags filled with beeswax candles and tied at the top with heavy twine. There should be a lot of dancing and an enormous bonfire after dark. Renaissance fairs and festivals are popular throughout the United States, and they are wonderful to attend if you're planning a Renaissance wedding, not only for costume and decoration ideas, but to purchase wedding-related items for sale at their booths. A great source of information is a publication entitled *Renaissance Magazine* which often profiles wedding vendors across the country who specialize in period weddings.

Celtic Theme

Celtic weddings have grown in popularity during the past five years and they usually include a bagpiper or a pipe band and period costumes. As with a Renaissance wedding, an outdoor setting or a castle is a lovely venue for a Celtic wedding, although any setting may be adaptable. The men may wear plaid tartans, kilts and traditional knee-high white socks and the bride may wear a period gown of heavy ivory satin with an elaborate brocaded bodice and a wreath of flowers and ribbons in her hair. Depending on the season, her attendants may wear deep green velvet gowns with tartan shawls or ivory organza gowns trimmed with matching lace. The bride may carry a decorated "lucky horseshoe" as she walks down the aisle, and children may ring tiny tinkling bells before the ceremony thought to ward off evil spirits. During the ceremony, the couple may participate in a "hand fasting" ritual, where the officiant binds the couple's right and left hands together with a cord, symbolizing the bond of marriage. Of course, the bride and groom are transported in a horse-drawn carriage.

Polynesian Theme

This theme works well around a swimming pool. Include Hawaiian music and hula dancers. Add Tiki torches, conch shells, Hawaiian fabrics, flower leis and colorful crepe paper flowers and garlands. Create "environmental" background music by playing tapes or CDs of real ocean sounds. Complete the ambience by floating rafts of fresh or crepe paper flowers in the pool and filling your buffet table with as much Polynesian fare as you can afford: roast pork, fresh pineapple, fresh coconut, grilled fish, melons, strawberries, loaves of sweet Hawaiian bread, sweet potatoes and, of course, bowls of poi (everyone loves to complain how it tastes like wallpaper paste!). Do you know anyone who can sing the Hawaiian Wedding Song?

Nostalgia Theme

Fill the reception site with memorabilia from the couple's past: baby photos; school awards; Little League uniform; cheerleading uniform; pom-poms; their high school and college yearbooks; dress up the couple's actual childhood teddy bears (if they still exist) as bride and groom. As you gather things from the bride's and groom's childhood and school years, more ideas will come to you, including something clever for the cake top: miniature megaphones with their school emblem? Tiny teddy bears dressed as bride and groom or, perhaps, dressed as cheerleader and football player? Use your imagination.

A Country-Western Roast

You can carry this theme as far as you like, decorating with lariats, cowboy hats, saddles, branding irons, singletrees, red bandanas, potted cactus plants and bales of hay. Cover your tables with checkered tablecloths and hire a country-western band, a country singer or play recorded country-western music. Give your reception a "roast theme" in every sense of the word, from barbecued foods to stand-up comedy as several friends and family members "roast" the bride and groom, using family photos, home movies, videos and true stories of embarrassing incidents. This idea works best for an informal outdoor reception in a park, in someone's oversized backyard or, ideally, at a working ranch. One bride even went so far as to make papier-mâché cowboy-boot centerpieces, miniature cowboy-hat favors filled with trail mix, and a "lasso-wrapped" wedding cake. As the coup de grace, see if you can round up a horse-drawn hay wagon as your getaway vehicle.

Mexican Fiesta Theme

Decorate with all the colorful and festive Mexican props you can find—huge crepe paper flowers, serapes, piñatas, the works! Do you have any friends who can play Mariachi music? If not, tapes and CDs are available at your public library.

Balloon Theme

The simple use of balloons, whether helium-filled or not, can create a stunning ambience all by themselves. Here are some clever ways to decorate with balloons:

❦ Bouquets

Add bouquets of helium-filled balloons throughout your reception site, as table centerpieces, colorful fillers "growing" up from the floor, tied to the backs of chairs or along banisters or railings, on windowsills, over doorways, to frame the bride and groom at the cake table or in the receiving line, or to create a "walkway" for the couple and their attendants to use as they enter the reception hall.

❦ Archways

Helium balloons, when attached to a fishing line held down at each end with heavy bricks, will form a natural arch by themselves! In fact with no help from you at all, they will actually *insist* on arching at the center, a convenient law of physics that will enable you to create archways over the head table, the receiving line, the cake table, or for the guests or wedding party to walk under as they enter the reception hall.

❦ Cover the Ceiling

Attach one helium-filled balloon to one regular balloon, tie them together with crinkle tie ribbon at their nipples, leaving several feet dangling down. Then, release them and let them float to the ceiling; when the reception is almost over and it's time for the bride and groom to make their escape, invite each guest to "catch" a balloon to take outside and release into the sky as the couple drives away.

Fifties Theme

Decorate the reception hall with fifties memorabilia, including Elvis posters, photographs of the parents or other relatives in their prom outfits or pictures of vintage fifties cars. Have a disc jockey do a "Wolf Man Jack" impression while playing fifties music. Top it off with a 1956 Cadillac convertible as the getaway car, trailing old shoes and tin cans. If you can't find a Cadillac, a '56 Chevy will do!

Are you getting the hang of it? Here are a few more theme party reception ideas:

Gay Nineties	Happy New Year
Roaring Twenties	Mississippi Riverboat
Renaissance Festival	Hollywood Movie Set
Tropical Rain Forest	Mountain Ski Resort
Carousel Horses	Beach Party
A Ship's Cruise	

Ceremony Themes

A ceremony theme is usually a little more formal than the reception theme, although it may be carried over to the reception if you'd like. Here are some of the more popular ceremony themes:

Costume Wedding

Costume weddings are very trendy these days. All you need is a theme that lends itself to costumes, such as: Henry VIII English Tudor; Renaissance; Medieval; Folk; Halloween; Masked Ball; Western; Polynesian; Guys 'n Dolls; Romeo & Juliet; Elizabethan; Victorian; Edwardian; Greco-Roman; Southern Antebellum; or any ethnic theme.

Costumes for these weddings may be sewn from patterns, rented from costume shops, borrowed from theatrical production companies, rented or purchased through catalogs available at many bridal salons.

Snowball Wedding

This is a wedding where all the women wear white, including the mothers and grandmothers, which projects a very elegant look to the ceremony. The men wear black tuxedos or white dinner jackets with black trousers. You may choose to decorate with white flowers and ribbon, as well, and include all-white bouquets for the women and boutonnieres for the men; however, I much prefer one dramatic shock of color splashed against the white, such as bright pink roses interspersed among the white arrangements with perhaps a touch of matching pink ribbon. It's a matter of personal taste, but the important thing is this: It's *imperative* that all the whites match! If they don't, the off-whites or ivories will appear to be dingy or dirty and the entire effect will be ruined. The smart thing is to let the bride select her gown first and match all the other whites to it, including the flowers, pew bows, candles, hairpieces, and even the aisle runner, if you choose to use one.

Black-and-White Wedding

All the wedding costumes are black and white. The men may wear black tuxes, the attendants black gowns with white trim, the flower girl white and the ring bearer black. This is a trendy theme these days, but be sure there's a little color splashed around somewhere or the wedding will lose its festive feeling. By the way, it's also trendy, and practical, for the bride's attendants to choose individual dresses of their own choice, just so they're black and white. This same idea works for a Navy Blue-and-White Wedding, as well.

Christmas Wedding

This is an easy theme to work with because of all the Christmas trees, holly, poinsettias and evergreenery available in December. Also, it's only natural to take advantage of all the tiny white Christmas tree lights that abound during the season, stringing them everywhere, creating a magical touch of winter wonderland.

Victorian Wedding

You can carry the Victorian theme as far as you like—all the way to period costumes and high-buttoned shoes if that appeals to you. Be sure to include plenty of lace, hearts, trailing ribbons, and you may want to create old-fashioned tussie-mussie bouquets for the bride and her attendants (a tussie mussie is a small cluster of flowers, tied with ribbons and tucked into an elegant silver or paper lace cone-shaped holder.) Shop garage sales and flea markets ahead of time for old-fashioned tea pots. Set one in the center of each table during the reception; fill the pots with delicate silk or fresh flowers, plus a little baby's breath and paper lace tucked in between the flowers. Tie each handle with a narrow satin ribbon.

> *Tip* These tea pots can double as gifts after the wedding, for your female helpers or members of your bridal party.

Candlelight Wedding

Plan an evening wedding that incorporates as many candles as you can afford, mounted in sconces on pillars, in candelabra, along window sills and altar railings, on tall candlesticks at the end of every other pew, and atop the organ and piano. Have your bridal attendants carry a single candle imbedded in an oasis filled with fresh flowers and, of course, include a traditional unity candle behind the altar. If you carry this theme through to your reception, you may want to give decorated candles as "favors" for the guests to light as you leave the reception, creating a glowing, romantic pathway from the reception site to your getaway vehicle.

The Home Wedding

More and more brides are choosing to be married at home in the presence of a limited number of close friends and family members, followed by a large reception at another site. The nice thing about a home wedding is that the natural charm and intimacy of the home itself offers a romantic ambience for the wedding; also, a home setting takes very little in the way of decorations. The first step is to unclutter the rooms: remove the oversized pieces of furniture (even if you only store them in the garage for the big day), and clear away most of the nicknacks, family photos, and so forth. This will leave room for white folding chairs, if you choose to use them, and a few small flower arrangements. The fireplace mantle may be decorated with greens, flowers, candles and ribbons and an altar can be created easily by covering any small, narrow table with a lace or damask tablecloth. By the way, if the room is too small for chairs, it's perfectly acceptable for the guests to stand during the ceremony. If you're marrying in the summer, you may decide to have the ceremony in the garden of your home, simplifying things all the more: you won't need any floral decorations; no heavy furniture to move; and no clutter to clear away.

An Indoor Garden Wedding

If you have your heart set on a garden wedding, but you're getting married in the winter, or you can't come up with an available garden for your ceremony, create the illusion of a garden indoors. This is easier than you might think. For starters, rent or borrow as much greenery as you can find (silk or fresh), from potted silk ficus trees, to potted patio shrubs and plants, to hanging fuchsia baskets, to ordinary house plants. As I've already mentioned, many nurseries will loan out or rent a designated number of potted bushes or trees for local weddings, but also scour the homes and patios of your close friends and family members, and while you're at it, keep an eye out for any portable trellises, arbors, white wrought iron benches or attractive wicker or white vinyl patio furniture. If you can't round up arbors and trellises, they're available for rent at many wedding supply stores, along with white picket fences, which really add a country garden ambience to the setting. Next, wind silk or fresh ivy and flowers around these props, tie them with bows and you'll have a lovely garden, regardless of the season. This is one of the easiest and most affordable themes, by the way.

Here are a few more theme possibilities:

Baskets of Flowers	Hearts
Wreaths	Flower Garden
Bells	Apple Blossoms
Golden Rings	Candles and Harps
Garden Trellises	Doves
Rose-Covered Arches	Parasols

For even more theme ideas, pick up a copy of my book entitled *Beautiful Wedding Decorations & Gifts on a Small Budget*.

Cost-Cutting Decorations

For our daughter's wedding and reception we came up with a "Winter Wonderland" theme. As I mentioned in the chapter on flowers, we used evergreen pine boughs from the "free florist" in the sanctuary and we also took advantage of Christmas decorations already provided by the church, including an enormous tree covered with thousands of white lights. The reception hall was filled with evergreen trees and shrubs loaned to us by a local nursery, along with pine boughs we strung together and draped everywhere we could. We trimmed all the trees and tables with large and small burgundy bows.

The ambience was primarily created by the free trees and shrubs, so our "big" expense was a $50 "ice sculpture" burgundy swan that became the centerpiece for the buffet table. We special-ordered this from the caterer, and it was a big hit. It sat in a bed of crushed ice that we covered with flowers from the produce department of the local supermarket. These flowers, by the way, cost a fraction of what they would cost at the retail florist and were very convenient for last-minute purchases.

Our main expenses in the sanctuary were the pew bows, which I made for $.70 each, and candles, $.49 each. Fortunately, the church had candle sconces already affixed to the sanctuary walls and pillars.

Our total expense for decorating the church and reception hall came to approximately $110. Everything else came from the "free florist."

You can keep your decorating expenses to a minimum by selecting a theme that lends itself to free and affordable props. Keep your eyes open for the following:

Traditional Themes

Wrought-iron or wooden benches

Nice lawn furniture (especially wicker)

Trellises

Latticework

Portable gazebos

Potted plants

Potted flowers (especially roses)

Potted shrubs, topiaries, trees

Bells of all types

Hearts

Love doves

Baskets

Dried grapevines

Wreaths of artificial flowers

Umbrellas of all sizes

Nontraditional Themes

Tiki torches

Old-fashioned decorative street lamps

Varied lighting, including strings of patio lights

Chinese lanterns

Posters

Wall hangings

Tropical plants

Sleigh bells

Skis, snowshoes, sleds

Wooden shoes, small windmills, potted tulips

Old South memorabilia

Gay nineties memorabilia

Fifties memorabilia

Costumes of all kinds

Antique clothes of all kinds

How to Tie Pew Bows

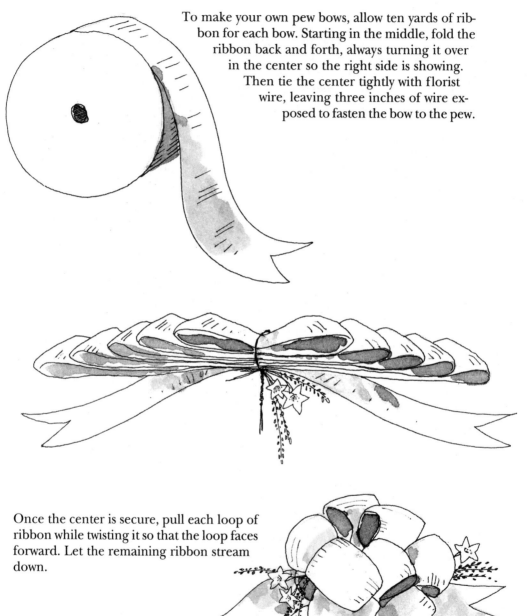

To make your own pew bows, allow ten yards of ribbon for each bow. Starting in the middle, fold the ribbon back and forth, always turning it over in the center so the right side is showing. Then tie the center tightly with florist wire, leaving three inches of wire exposed to fasten the bow to the pew.

Once the center is secure, pull each loop of ribbon while twisting it so that the loop faces forward. Let the remaining ribbon stream down.

If you begin watching for these props a year or so in advance of your wedding, you should have plenty of time to collect everything you need. However, if you only have a few months to plan your reception, you'll need to choose a theme that requires props you already have on hand or can round up quickly from friends and family.

As an example, you may have a loving and adoring aunt and uncle with a Shangri-la backyard full of archways, trellises, wrought-iron park benches, elegant lawn furniture, portable pots of flowers, trees and shrubs, strings of Victorian patio lights, hanging flower baskets, and several decorative street lamps. Depending on just how loving and adoring they are, you may have your entire reception decor right there. If not, they may be happy to loan you a good part of it or, if you're very lucky, they may even offer to host your reception in their backyard.

Another source of reception props are garage sales. It's amazing what people are trying to sell at these things, especially if they're moving.

You can always rent a little ambience, too. Here are typical rental prices for props that may help out.

White picket fencing, 2' × 4'	$ 3.50 ea.
Lattice trellis	70.00
Lattice screens	40.00
Urns	12.00/pair
Wishing well	12.00
Kneeling bench	18.00
Gazebo	140.00
Canopy, 20' × 20'	225.00
Carousel horses	45.00
Garden tables and umbrellas	25.00
Mirror ball with lights	40.00
Dance floors, 12' × 15'	200.00
Helium tanks for filling balloons (will fill three hundred large balloons)	35.00
Champagne fountain	42.00
White plastic folding chairs	1.30 ea.
Pillars	15.00/pair
Flowers urns	15.00/pair
9-light candelabra	24.00/pair
Large white bird cage	18.00
9' white, free-standing umbrella	32.00
Decorated wedding arch	30.00
Money tree	12.00

After you've borrowed or rented everything you can round up, you'll still need to purchase a few things. Here is a sample shopping list:

Crepe paper streamers, 500′	$ 7.25
Crepe paper sheets	3.00
Candles, 12″	.65 ea.
Candles, 18″	.80 ea.
Ice molds	38.00
Balloons, helium	.90 ea.
Balloons, regular (package of 100)	.10 ea.
2″ Ribbon, 100 yards	12.25
1″ Ribbon, 100 yards	8.50
Posterboard	1.30
Grapevine wreaths, undecorated	7.50

Keep thinking "free," "borrowed" and "on sale," and you'll have all the ambience you can handle well within your budget.

9
Say Cheese!

(Capture the Memories at Affordable Prices)

The day after the wedding can be a bit of a letdown to the families of the bride and groom. The cake is a memory, the guests have gone home and the flowers are as tired as the mother of the bride. There is a delightful cure, however, for these post-wedding blues: the wedding captured in photos and videotape.

A videotape of the wedding and reception will bring instant delight. Even as the loving couple enjoys their honeymoon, families and friends can be reliving the happy day. And since it doesn't have to be processed, a videotape can be replayed immediately—just settle back in your favorite chair and enjoy the fruits of your labors.

The photographs require more time because they must be processed and printed, but they, too, will capture the memories. The average cost of wedding photography in this country is about $1,500, which provides a basic wedding package which may consist of four 8×10s, forty 4×5s and a leather album. You'll pay extra for the bride's engagement portrait, the parents' albums, additional prints, and so forth.

If you're like most couples, you'll want to have your wedding videotaped as well, which means an additional $1,000 or so. A $1,000 basic package usually consists of one videographer with one video camera for two hours, and no special effects. If you want more hours, or you want two camera coverage, plus special editing, you'll pay more for each of these extras. A few of the special editing features available are such things as a visit to the bride's home on the morning of the wedding, a photo montage of the couple's baby pictures, guest interviews during the reception, personalized graphics, commentary, background music and a condensed version of ceremony and reception highlights at the end of the tape. By the way, each of these features may be priced at individual add-on prices.

Now for the good news: I have several ways for you to save on the photography and videography. Let's start with the photography.

Cost-Cutting Photography Plans

Amateur Photographer

Approximate Cost *$93*

Under this plan, we're assuming you have a friend or relative who takes pretty good pictures, has the right kind of camera and, most important, agrees to photograph your wedding for free. The $93 will cover the film, developing, and printing of approximately 192 pictures. A roll of 24-exposure Kodak color film for a 35mm camera will cost about $1.62 per roll (an eight-pack of 24-exposure Kodak film at Target is a total of $12.99). The developing of this film, plus printing of 5 × 7s, will cost approximately $10 per roll, also at Target. It's wise to have all the film developed in 5 × 7s, otherwise, at a later date, each 5 × 7 will cost about $2.50 per print. So, by having all the rolls developed in 5 × 7s from the start, it will be like having free proofs. By the way, for only a few dollars more, you can get double 5 × 7 prints at the time the film is developed. So, if you use all eight rolls of 24-exposure film, you'll have 192 prints, for a total cost of about $93, and this low cost even includes the negatives, plus extra 5 × 7s for the parents' albums.

So, what's the catch to this unbelievably affordable photography plan? The catch is that you need an amateur photographer with some degree of savvy, plus—and this is the important part—the photographer must have a quality camera with features at least as good as those listed under the "Rented Camera" plan.

What about the risk, you ask? What if your amateur photographer totally blows it and none of the prints turn out? After all, there's no "do overs"—the day is history and you'll never get married again. So, what precautions can be taken to prevent this disaster? Here are a few guidelines:

Guidelines for Using Amateur Photographers

1. Ask two or more amateur photographers to take pictures. Provide film for all of them. Surely, some of the pictures will turn out.

2. Request the amateurs follow my "Tips for Amateurs" at the end of this section. I have gleaned expert advice from some of the top wedding photographers in the country.

3. Be sure to have your wedding videographed also. This will provide an added assurance that you'll have your day captured on film. If none of the still pictures turn out, there is a procedure whereby you can have photographs created from a videotape. The "freeze-frame" technique is used to print each image desired. This is the procedure used in police work to create a still photo from a videotape of a criminal at work. This is not to suggest that you expect any nefarious guests at your wedding, but it's a comforting emergency option just in case none of the still photography turns out.

4. Make up a list of "must" shots for your amateur, and provide a helper who will assemble the guests for these shots. The helper should be someone who knows the family members by name. See the sample list of "must" shots at the end of this chapter. They were suggested to me by a well-known wedding photographer. Use the list for ideas, but add your own special shots.

5. A final safeguard is to supply some of your guests with disposable cameras. Have a basketful at the door when your guests arrive. These one-time-use cameras are combination camera-and-film-in-one. A roll of twenty-seven with flash is about $14. Encourage your guests to click away; then collect the mini-cameras as the guests leave. This will not only assure you of *some* kind of still photos, but you'll have interesting candid shots you wouldn't have had otherwise. By the way, Kodak now offers a "Wedding Party Pack" of five throwaway flash cameras for approximately $45.

On behalf of amateur photographers everywhere, I would like to give a word of praise. When my husband and I were married we hired a professional photographer who did not get a single picture of our wedding because his film was bad. The only memories we have of our wedding are an excellent home movie taken by my husband's uncle and various snapshots taken by the guests. If it weren't for these amateurs who did such a good job, we wouldn't have any photos at all. By the way, we have since had the delightful movie transferred to a videotape, with extra copies for our children. Hurray for the amateur!

Amateur With Rented Camera
Approximate Cost *$163*

Very often an amateur photographer does not have the proper camera needed to photograph a wedding. Even though he may own a fine camera, it may not have an extended flash arm or gel cell capability, for example. In this case, just rent one from a large camera store. I checked prices all over the country and it will cost you about $70 to rent the following equipment:

> One 35mm, fully automatic camera. It must have a flash arm that is at least eight inches away from the lens. The best brands are Canon, Minolta, Nikon or Pentax.

> One wide-angled lens.

> One fully charged gel cell for power. (This eliminates the problem of replacing batteries during the day.)

Arrange for your amateur to go to the camera shop to pick up the equipment personally. This way the staff can explain the camera's features and prevent unpleasant surprises later. As an extra precaution, the amateur should take a roll of film with the camera before the wedding day, to become as familiar as possible with its features.

The film can be taken to a one-hour photo lab so the prints can be analyzed in plenty of time.

Artistry Only
Approximate Cost *$450*

There is a relatively unknown service offered by a very few professional photographers. The professional comes to the wedding, uses his or her own camera and film and charges only for shooting the pictures. At the end of the day the photographer turns all the film over to the bride's family who will have it processed at a later date. Usually, the reason the photographer can afford to work this way is because he works out of his home and doesn't have the expense of a fancy studio.

The advantages of this plan are obvious: you have a professional artist experienced in wedding photography with his or her own camera and film; you are relieved of the fear that the pictures won't turn out.

The disadvantage of this plan is that you may be getting an inferior photographer. Some say that photographers who work this way do so because they aren't good enough to establish a full-service business.

On the other hand, there are many satisfied customers of this type of "Artistry Only" plan. Ask for referrals; look at the photographer's work. If you feel confident, go ahead. In my hometown there are two excellent photographers who will work this way.

Find a Reasonable Photographer
Approximate Cost *$800*

Photography prices vary considerably depending on the artistic reputation of the photographer. The trick is to find a wonderful photographer whose reputation hasn't caught up with his or her artistic ability—one who does excellent work, but still charges a reasonable price. You do this by asking around; check with other mothers of the bride, other recent brides, your neighbors and friends. Try to line one up six months before the wedding, or as soon as you have set the date.

This is the route we took with our daughter's wedding. We were fortunate to find an excellent photographer who charged us $500 for a package that included:

❧ Four hours of unlimited photography

❧ A minimum of 125 preview prints

❧ One bride's album containing thirty 8×10 prints

The purchase of the remaining preview prints, the parents' albums and all other special orders were extra. This plan worked out well for us because it gave us a chance to catch our breath after the wedding and save a little money toward our own album, which we purchased four months later.

We were very pleased with our photographer, who was not only artistically qualified, but calm, organized, personable and helpful. His wife accompanied him and carefully checked off the "must" shots as they were taken. They both had pleasant personalities and were a pleasure to have present on our special day.

If you decide to go with this plan, just a word of caution: get everything in writing. When will the previews be ready? Does the price include an album? If so, what quality? Exactly how many photos will be included in the album and what size? How many hours of photography are included in the price? When will the photographer arrive? I don't mean to frighten you—I just don't want you to end up in front of Judge Judy. You know what she would ask: "Did you get the agreement in writing?"

> ***Tip*** While you're getting bids from professional photographers, ask how much you can save by having your wedding photographed in black-and-white.

If you have trouble finding a reasonably-priced photographer, go to PrimeShot (www.primeshot.com) who can provide you with quotes for certified photographers who shoot weddings for 20 percent to 30 percent less than studio photographers.

Photograph the Ceremony Only
Approximate Cost *$500*

One popular option is to hire a professional photographer for the ceremony only, leaving the rest of the photography to talented amateurs. This plan has a lot of merit because the reception will likely have a lot of videotaping going on, which will provide the additional assurance of still photos from the videotapes, just in case the amateurs blow their assignments! By the way, these still photos have come down in price the last few years and only run about $15 each.

Tips for Amateur Photographers

1. When using a 35mm camera, be aware that, unless your camera features a through-the-lens viewfinder, the image you see when you snap the picture is not what will be printed in the photograph. Allow extra width for group pictures. The print may be cropped on the sides cutting off the persons on the ends unless you have plenty of "air" around the group.

2. Avoid "red-eye," the eerie glow in a photo subject's eyes caused by having the flash too close to the lens. Be sure your flash is mounted, with a simple bracket, at least eight inches away from the lens. Other ways to avoid this annoying result is to have the subjects look off to the left or right of the camera or look toward the bride or another object, such as the bride's ring

Good and Bad Group Photo Placements

WRONG: For group portraits, don't line the wedding party up like tin soldiers, with all the men on one side and the women on the other. Although this is a standard placement, it's not very interesting.

RIGHT: Create visual interest by using steps to stagger the heights of the wedding party. Alternate the men and women, and seat the flower girl and ring bearer at the feet of the bride and groom.

or flowers. Be especially careful with children because they tend to look straight at a camera. It is also possible to reduce "red-eye" by using a camera that has a "double-flash" feature, as most brand-name cameras now do. This feature is very helpful to the amateur photographer. "Red-eye" is caused by the reflection of light from the pupil of the eye, but with "double-flash," the first flash causes the pupil to become smaller so that less light is reflected. The second flash goes off when the picture is actually being taken, thus reducing "red-eye." In other words, the first flash "tricks" the pupil into closing, the second flash takes a picture with a natural appearance.

3. Be wary of backgrounds. Watch for peculiar shapes that may look like a branch growing out of someone's head or a statue sitting on the groom's shoulder. Try to keep backgrounds as uncluttered as possible.

4. Be aware of light conditions. If you're taking outdoor shots, do not force people to look into the sun—they will squint. Face them away from the sun. And be careful not to have the bride standing in full sun while the groom is in shadow. Keep the light exposure uniform. When photographing indoors watch for the possibility of underexposure. The bride's white dress or the white frosting on the wedding cake are the two greatest enemies of your light meter. To "trick" your camera in these two cases, take your camera off "automatic" and focus on the bride's face, then "exposure lock" this setting. This will prevent underexposure of the subjects' faces, even when you stand back to take the picture.

5. When posing the subjects, avoid lining them up like "tin soldiers." Group them in a natural way, placing heavyset or tall people in the rear. Stairways are natural settings for group shots. Most important, count to three, instructing them to keep their eyes open on "three." The biggest problem with group pictures is that someone will blink. After you've taken the picture, *ask* if anyone blinked. They'll usually be honest enough to tell you so you can take the shot again. By the way, be sure that the bride and groom are *always* in the forefront or at the top of any picture.

6. Capture emotions and relationships with close-ups and candid shots. Don't be afraid to come in very tight on a shot, framing only the faces of the bride and groom, for instance. And watch for hugging, touching and meaningful looks, not only between the bride and groom, but between mother and daughter or father and son. The bride and groom will appreciate the thoughtfulness of tender close-ups and candid spontaneity.

7. Be careful in the use of the flash. Check with the clergyman ahead of time to see if a flash is allowed in church. If so, only use it when the father walks the bride up the aisle and the groom walks her back down. Otherwise, use natural light with timed exposures during the ceremony.

8. Don't accidentally use up all your film on the ceremony; save plenty for the reception. It can't hurt to have a few extra rolls of film "just in case."

9. Be sensitive to people's unattractive features. For example, if the groom's mother has a banana nose that dangles over her upper lip, don't shoot her from the side; likewise, don't take a front shot of the best man if his ears stick out like satellite dishes.

10. Being an amateur, you can avoid a lot of stress by planning to take as many pictures as possible before the ceremony begins. Even if the bride doesn't want the groom to see her before the wedding, she can still have her picture taken with her mother, maid of honor, father, grandmother, and so forth. The same is true of the groom. Many of the "must" shots can be gotten out of the way, relieving the pressure of having to take too many shots between the ceremony and the reception. Take every formal photo possible before the wedding; this will alleviate stress after the ceremony.

11. Be a nice guy or gal. Try to be mellow, pleasant and unobtrusive. Don't boss anyone around. Make friendly suggestions, and compliment the people you are trying to photograph. They'll relax and pose much more naturally with this approach. Your overall attitude will have an effect on everyone concerned. If you're loud and frenzied, everyone around you will become that way too. A quiet, polite photographer can have a calming effect on the entire event.

You will, of course, want to make up your own unique list of "must" shots (see below). There will be special people or events you will want photographed, especially in the case of an ethnic wedding. You can copy the list that follows or make up your own personalized list for your notebook. Be sure to give a copy of the list to your photographer at least a week before the wedding.

Suggested Must Shots

Bride

Bride finishing makeup
Bride with bouquet
Bride's mother or maid of honor helping with veil
Bride with mother
Bride with father
Bride with both parents
Bride with her grandparents
Bride with the children in the wedding
Bride—full length portrait
Bride with bridesmaids
Bride with groomsmen
Bride with maid or matron of honor

Groom

Groom with his parents
Groom with his mother
Groom with his father
Groom with his grandparents
Groom with the children in the wedding
Groom with groomsmen
Groom with bridesmaids
Groom with best man

Ceremony

Bride and father walking up the aisle
Timed exposures:
    Kneeling in prayer
    Lighting unity candle
    Exchanging vows
    Kiss
Bride and groom walking down the aisle

After the Ceremony

Several shots of bride and groom
Bride and groom with both sets of parents
Bride and groom with entire wedding party

Reception

Special decorations, food displays, etc.
Couple arriving at reception
Bride and groom's first dance
Bride dancing with her father
Groom dancing with his mother
Best man's toast
Bride and groom cutting cake
Bride and groom feeding each other cake
Close-up of rings on hands of bride and groom
Bride throwing her bouquet
Groom taking off bride's garter
Groom throwing the garter
Bride and groom with those who caught the bouquet and garter
Throwing rice or bird seed
Bride and groom waving as they get into car

The Latest Trends in Candid Photography

As I mentioned in my Introduction, candid wedding photography has become very popular, often in preference to formal shots altogether. Here are some candid ideas:

🐦 A touching shot of the bride and her father at home

🐦 An outdoor shot with a sunrise or sunset in the background

🐦 A shot of the bride and groom at a nearby park or swinging on their childhood swings

🐦 If the wedding is held on a ranch or out in the country, a shot of the bride and groom sitting on a fence with their arms around the necks of a couple horses

🐦 A shot of the bride's and groom's empty wedding shoes, sitting side by side

🐦 If it's a rainy day, a humorous shot of the bride and groom "singing in the rain" while dancing with an umbrella

🐦 If it's a winter wedding with plenty of snow on the ground, a shot of the bride and groom with their arms around a snowman, built ahead of time by the members of the wedding party and decorated with a top hat and scarf in the wedding colors

🐦 A real tight close-up shot of the bride's and groom's faces during their first dance

🐦 A close-up shot of the couple saying goodbye to their parents after the reception

🐦 The couple with their arms around one of their pets that has been decked out ahead of time in the wedding colors

Cost-Cutting Videography Plans

Videography, or videotaping, has become so affordable these days, and at least one person in every family seems to have a decent video camera for recording special events. For the price of a good videotape, you can have hours of live recording, complete with voices, music, sounds and antics. There isn't anyone who doesn't enjoy watching himself "on television." It holds people's interest by the hour.

My daughter and son-in-law had their wedding professionally videotaped as a wedding gift. Because of this person's generosity, we have some very dear, poignant moments recorded forever, complete with the sounds of our daughter's laughter, the chimes on the organ, and Dad's quavering voice as he gave his daughter away. A videotape, even one made by an amateur, will become a family treasure. I've even spoken with brides who say that if they had to choose between videotape and photographs, they would pick videotape. Photographs are works of art, but videotapes are addictive entertainment!

So, I presume you'll want your wedding taped, and I can't blame you. Here are some affordable ideas:

Amateur Videographer
Approximate Cost *$15*

Find a friend or relative with a quality video camera, a camera with features at least as nice as the ones described in the next plan, "Amateur With Rented Camera." If possible, view some of the videotapes made by this person. If the tapes look good and you feel comfortable asking, drop a gentle hint. Perhaps this amateur will offer to tape the whole wedding and reception as a wedding gift.

If you have two or three friends with cameras who offer to tape your day, take them up on it. It would be nice to have at least two cameras taping during the ceremony. One could tape from the rear and one from the front, tastefully hidden from view. This would provide close-ups of the bride and groom. You would, of course, have an additional cost for each videotape used.

Under this amateur videography plan you'll be left with unedited tape, which means you don't have any of the special embellishments the professionals can add, such as graphics or commentary, but you can hardly complain about the cost! And because it's much easier to videotape a wedding than it is to photograph it, there is less chance of serious error. A photographer must assemble and pose his subjects and there's always the possibility that someone will blink, spoiling the shot. With videotaping, however, it's no problem; there is no posing or positioning—it's a spontaneous recording of events as they happen. Just be sure to have your amateurs look over the "Tips for Amateur Videographers" at the end of this chapter.

Amateur With Rented Camera
Approximate Cost *$65*

If you have a willing videographer who has no camera, rent one. The average cost to rent a quality camera is about $50. This, added to the cost of the tape, will bring your total to about $65. Rent a camera with these features:

- ❦ Portable

- ❦ Battery-operated

🐝 Half-inch color camera with recorder

🐝 Fully automatic with playback

🐝 One tripod

You'll also want to rent two battery packs that have been fully charged. And, as with the rented still camera, be sure to have your amateur try out the camera in advance.

Two Amateurs With Rented Cameras
Approximate Cost *$130*

As I've already mentioned, it's better to have two cameras. If you have two willing amateurs, it will only cost you $50 more to rent two cameras instead of one. This will provide that important coverage at the front of the church during the ceremony.

There is also the safety factor: It's better to have two people videotaping than one, just in case one person misses something or has problems with the camera, batteries or film.

Find a Reasonable Videographer
Approximate Cost *$500*

Prices vary so drastically that it isn't difficult to find a videographer who will make a two-hour tape, non-edited, for $500. It's true that most charge about $1,000 for this same package, but you can find it for less if you ask around. In our town, for example, we have a major university with a lot of hungry students, some of whom will gladly videotape a wedding for less than $500. I've seen some of their work, and it's excellent. You find out about these people by talking to other brides or by calling a university's Telecommunications Department or Instructional Materials Center. You can also give your local TV stations a call because cameramen often moonlight doing weddings. Whoever you hire, however, just be sure to get your agreement in writing!

Tips for Amateur Videographers

1. Move the camera *SLOWLY!* When panning during the reception, for example, move the camera so slowly and steadily that it seems like "overkill." Use the tripod whenever possible to avoid jerky movements and remember that even your breathing can cause a "heaving" motion in the camera.

2. Likewise, zoom in and out very *SLOWLY!* A professional videotape never has any jerky motion—everything is smooth. Try your hardest to keep all camera movements as slow and smooth as possible.

3. Get close-ups of as many people as you can. The wide-angle shot is useful to establish the setting, but the close-ups are the most appreciated. Hold the camera on each shot to a minimum count of "five"; "ten" is even better. Counting to five will seem too long to you at the time, but is just right when viewing the tape later. Just remember that you are the viewers' "eyes." Don't make them seasick with sudden, jerky movements.

4. Some of the most charming tapes have live interviews with family, friends, the minister, best man, maid of honor, the bride and groom. These interviews will bring tears and laughter in the years to come. By the way, don't ask typical plain vanilla questions such as, "Do you have anything you would like to say to the bride and groom?" or "Do you have a greeting for the bride and groom?" Instead, ask "open-ended" questions; for example, you might ask the mother of the bride, "When did you first meet your son-in-law? What was your first impression of him?" Likewise, ask the mother of the groom about the bride: "When did you first meet her?" Ask the father of the bride: "Did the groom ask you for your daughter's hand in marriage? Where were you when this happened?" Ask the bride: "How did he propose to you? Where were you? How long had you known him?" Ask Grandma: "Did you enjoy the music? What did you think of your granddaughter as she walked down the aisle?" Ask the maid of honor: "How long have you known the bride? What did you two do for fun back when you were first friends?" Ask the best man: "How long have you known the groom? Did you play sports together? Do you have any tricks planned for later? I noticed that you decorated their car."

Interview the brothers and sisters, too. Try to get them talking about their relationships with each other and things they did together when they were growing up. Do some investigative work ahead of time; know who people are and try to have some personalized questions ready. Write your questions out so that you'll have them handy at the reception.

5. Practice using the camera before the wedding. Be sure that it's working properly and try using the "smooth and slow" approach.

6. Only tape on "SP," (the two-hour speed). This will give you a much better quality picture. Keep an extra videotape on hand in case you need it.

7. Try to be as inconspicuous as possible; nothing is more obnoxious than a videographer who comes on strong and attracts attention with his "party personality." Keep it low-key!

Thanks for the Memories

The day after our daughter's wedding we sat and watched the videotape; how glad I was to have the memories recorded in such a meaningful way. I watched myself on the tape as I teased my daughter in the dressing room before the wedding. As I slipped a wedding slipper onto her foot, I asked her if it fit. She said, "Yes, of course." I said, "Oh, good. Since the shoe fits, you *must* be Cinderella!" I was desperately trying to lighten things up. She was getting nervous and, although I was trying not to show it, my stomach was fluttering, too. The feeling of that moment, along with all the others, will be there to recall for a lifetime.

When the photographer's preview prints were finally ready, we reveled in the joy of selecting favorites for our albums. I spent many quiet moments with a cup of tea beside me and a kitty in my lap, savoring and reliving the precious memories of that day. You'll want to capture your memories, too, so try for as many as you can—they're the perfect cure for those post-wedding blues!

> ***Tip*** You can also share the wedding photos online by scanning them yourself, or by using one of the free sites, such as Picturetrail (www.pi cturetrail.com). Or, you can share the photos with your friends and family members by having your negatives processed into digital images by AOL's "You've Got Pictures" or Kodak's "Photonet."

10
Potpourri

(Keeping Costs Down on All Those Little Extras)

The dictionary calls "potpourri" a "miscellaneous collection," and that's exactly what I have for you in this chapter. These are the extra expenses that don't seem to fall into any of the other categories, but can really hit you unexpectedly if you aren't ready for them! Many of these "annoying pests" pop up near the end, when you think you've overcome the worst! It's just like running a race, only to discover that you can't get to the finish line without passing through a swarm of angry yellow jackets. But, have no fear, this chapter will prepare you for this encounter!

I've divided these expenses into two categories: those you'll probably have to face, and those you can probably do without. When we figure your budget in chapter thirteen, I'll always be referring to the first category. Record these expenses in your notebook under "Incidentals."

Extra Expenses You'll Probably Have to Face
Rental of Ceremony and Reception Sites
Approximate Cost . . . . $0–$800

Before we consider the costs of ceremony and reception sites, you should be aware of these general, common-sense considerations:

❧ When setting your wedding date, avoid May to October if at all possible (the priciest time of year for weddings).

❧ Schedule your wedding for Friday or Sunday, both of which cost far less than Saturday, especially Saturday night.

❧ Consider an alfresco (outdoor) wedding and reception, avoiding the cost of a hall or banquet room altogether.

❦ The most desirable, yet affordable, sites are booked at least a year in advance, so make this one of your first decisions.

When it comes to the costs of the sites themselves, let me say that I'm well aware of the exorbitant rental fees being charged around the country, and I know many of your friends are paying these fees without a second thought. Some of these pricier choices include:

❦ Country clubs

❦ Resorts

❦ Hotel ballrooms

❦ Restaurants

❦ Country inns

Not only are most of these facilities quite expensive to rent, but they usually require you to order your reception food off their menu, at their prices, hire their waiters and bartenders, purchase their champagne, order your wedding cake from their bakery, pay their staff to cut and serve it, and also hire the rest of their employees as well, including coat attendants, parking valets, coordinators, and florists. As you can imagine, once you've totaled all these expenses, the facility rental fee is the least of your worries.

So, what is the answer? The answer is to rent a site that is not only affordable, but gives *you* control: to provide your own home-cooked food or hire your own caterer; purchase your own champagne from Price Club by the case; allow your aunt to bake your wedding cake and let your friends cut and serve it, if that's what you choose to do. Fortunately, the most affordable wedding sites are usually those that give you this control, including these choices:

❦ *Your Own Church or Synagogue*
As far as your ceremony is concerned, your own church or synagogue is probably available to you at very little cost; that is, if you choose to have a formal ceremony in a place of worship. By the way, according to a recent poll taken by *Bride's* magazine, 87 percent of all formal weddings take place in a church, synagogue or chapel. The average cost is $250 if you are a member, if not, it's $750. Then, if you're lucky, there may also be a social hall that can be used for your reception.

❦ *Historical Sites*
Historical buildings, such as nineteenth-century libraries or school-

houses, provide a setting which will make your wedding unique and special. (Call your local Historical Society for suggestions.)

🐦 City, County or State Facilities
Local and state governments offer some surprising choices, such as senior centers, parks, rose gardens, museums of natural history, library or courthouse grounds, marinas, clubhouses, and university or college facilities. The book *Bridges of Madison County* spurred a trend of weddings on bridges. And in California, one wedding took place in the shadow of a giant steam locomotive in the California State Railroad Museum in Sacramento; another at the sumptuous Japanese Pavilion and Gardens at Micke Grove Park near Stockton; and still another at the boat house at Oak Grove Regional Park, where the total rental fee was under $100 for six hours, plus gate fees.

🐦 Sites Available Through the Chamber of Commerce
Your local Chamber of Commerce may have a list of sites, some of which are quite affordable, such as private mansions, art galleries, Elks halls, private wedding chapels, privately-owned gardens, ranches or farms, yachts, botanical gardens, arboretums, clubhouses belonging to gated and retirement communities, and private campgrounds. Also check the yellow pages and ask around.

🐦 National Parks
The federal government allows outdoor weddings to be performed in its national parks, as well. Yosemite Park in California, for example, only requires a permit which costs less than $50, available from the Chief Ranger. The purpose of the permit, according to their public information officer, is to "keep track of where people get married and to be sure no two weddings are scheduled for the same time and place."

🐦 Other Interesting Public and Private Sites
Wedding ceremonies are also being held in corporate conference rooms, private homes and gardens, hilltops, meadows, on golf course putting greens, at the seashore, on docked ferries, at the top of ski slopes, in lobbies of commercial buildings and alongside mountain streams. Look for the book entitled *Places: A Directory of Public Places for Private Events and Private Places for Public Functions*, published by Tenth House Enterprises, New York City. This fascinating book lists a variety of wedding and reception sites throughout the country, including such places as the Discovery Cove Building

at the New York Aquarium which throws in a free sea lion and walrus show with each wedding.

Invitations
Approximate Cost . . . . *$.75 × 175 = $131.25*

You can pay from $2.00 to $10.00 per invitation retail, but this low price of only $.75 includes an inner and outer envelope, the invitation, and tissue inserts, and printing at a quick-print shop. In order to get the cost down this far, you must purchase these sets from a paper supply store. They'll come blank—without any printing on them.

Bring the quick-print copy shop a good laser-printed original of your wording or a copy prepared by a calligrapher and you won't be charged the additional typesetting fee.

There are also discount printers who can provide invitations at this low cost, sometimes by mail order. Good sources for these mail-order houses are the advertisements in bridal magazines; most offer a free catalog with prices up to 50 percent off retail.

> *Tip* I've found an excellent software program for creating your own invitations, called the "Wedding Invitation Kit" which costs about $24.99 in your local Michaels arts and crafts store. The kit includes the software, a wedding planner, guest list database, twenty-five invitations/envelopes, fifty note cards, plus response cards, and thank-yous.

> *Tip* Discounted invitations are also available through Discount Bridal Service (see Resources on pages 176-179).

Thank-You Notes
Approximate Cost . . . . *$.50 × 100 gifts = $50*

The etiquette books say that thank-you notes only need to be plain white and, preferably, written with a fine-point black pen. The notes do not need to be engraved with initials. Therefore, buy them in bulk from the paper supply house and save that big expense.

Postage
Approximate Cost . . . *$.37 × 175 invitations = $64.75*

Unfortunately we have to pay Uncle Sam or he won't deliver our invitations. The only alternative is to hand deliver as many as appropriate; for example, relatives and very close friends. Otherwise, it's proper etiquette to send them through the snail mail.

Mail-Order Invitations

Pamela
and
Jay

Mr. and Mrs. Morris Samuelsen
and
Mr. Howard Peyton
request the honour of your presence
as their children
Pamela Jean
and
Jay Joel
share the Sacrament of Matrimony
A Wedding Mass will celebrate this union
Saturday, the twentieth of October
Nineteen hundred and ninety
at ten o'clock in the morning
St. Bonaventure Catholic Church
16400 Springdale Street
Huntington Beach, California

Rexcraft No. 2258

Mr. and Mrs. Lester Vincent Doyle
request the honour of your presence
at the marriage of their daughter
Paige Allison
to
Mr. Frederick Brian Gregory
Saturday, the seventh of April
Nineteen hundred and ninety
at seven o'clock in the evening
Church of the Savior
4244 Genessee Boulevard
Aurora, Colorado

Sugar 'n Spice No. 262

Many companies offer a variety of beautiful yet inexpensive wedding invitations by mail order. Most have toll-free numbers and will send free catalogs and samples. Check recent issues of bridal magazines for advertisements and see the Resources section on pages 176-179.

Blood Test for Bride
Approximate Cost *$50*

This charge varies from state to state. It can be as low as $15 through county health services or a student's health service on a college campus. Some states don't even require a blood test. The groom pays for his own test.

Marriage License
Approximate Cost *$35*

This fee varies from state to state and county to county.

Favors
Approximate Cost . . . . *$.53 × 150 = $79.50*

After a lot of research, I came up with ten inexpensive favors that you can make yourself. You generally only give favors to female guests so you'll need approximately 150 for a wedding of 300 guests. Most of the supplies listed below can be purchased at a floral or craft supply house. Here they are:

Blue Net With Almonds

Tie blue tulle (thin netting) around two or three Jordan almonds, securing with narrow ribbon. As you tie the bow, include a small pearl heart.

Bag of 400 Jordan almonds	$17.49
One roll tulle (cut 6″×6″)	14.69
150 small pearl hearts	13.99
One roll narrow ribbon (100 yards)	9.00
Total	$55.17

(This will make 150 favors @ $.37 each.)

Almond Favors With Dove

Wrap three almonds with the netting rounds. Wire one dove around the top and tie with double ribbons.

Bag of 400 Jordan almonds	$17.49
Three bags netting rounds	33.00
One bag doves on wire	12.55
Two rolls ribbon	18.00
Total	$81.04

(This will make 133 favors @ $.61 each.)

Champagne Glasses With Almonds

Fill champagne glass with two or three almonds and cover top with tulle, bringing it down to the stem of the glass. Secure with ribbon and a tiny silk flower.

150 small plastic champagne glasses*	$35.70
Bag of 400 Jordan almonds	17.49
One roll tulle	9.00
One roll (100 yards) + 10 yards ribbon	15.00
Four stems silk flowers	6.00
Total	$83.19

(This will make 150 favors @ $.55 each.)

* Available through party supply stores and Web sites, such as Oriental Trading Company (see Resources on pages 176-179)

Netted Soaps

Purchase decorative soaps at $.50 each. Tie them up with tulle and ribbon with double-bows.

150 soaps	$75.00
One roll tulle	9.00
One roll (100 yards) + 10 yards ribbon	15.00
Total	$99.00

(This will make 150 favors @ $.66 each.)

Netted Potpourri

Buy sacks of herbs and spices and enclose small portions in tulle netting. Tie with ribbon and one flower.

Two pounds potpourri	$42.00
One roll tulle	9.00
One roll narrow ribbon (100 yards)	15.00
Four stems silk flowers	6.00
Total	$72.00

(This will make 150 favors @ $.48 each.)

Netted Bird Seed

Throwing rice has passed out of fashion; it evidently can make birds very sick because they eat too much and it swells in their stomachs. So, it's become popular to throw bird seed instead. Wrap golf ball-size portions of seed in net; tie with ribbon and a tiny silk flower.

Twenty-four pounds bird seed*	$ 8.00
One roll tulle	9.00
One roll narrow ribbon	15.00
Four stems silk flowers	6.00
Total	$38.00

(This will make 150 favors @ $.25 each.)

   * The Home Depot sells bird seed in 20-lb. sacks for only $3.97 each.

   The guests, of course, aren't required to untie the favors and toss the bird seed at the bride and groom—they may take them home if they wish.

Decorated Candles

Decorate the "handle" or bottom of an eight-inch candle with tufted netting and tiny silk flowers. At the end of the reception give one to each guest to light and use to form a "get-away" path for the bride and groom; this idea only works, of course, for an evening wedding.

Two rolls tulle netting	$ 18.00
150 8″ candles	102.00
Four stems silk flowers (approximately forty tiny blooms to tie or glue to the tulle base)	6.00
Total	$126.00

(This will make 150 favors @ $.84 each.)

Decorated Seed Packets With Notes Attached

Give each guest a decorated packet of seeds with a personalized note attached which reads something like this: "As these seeds bloom into flowers, may they remind you of how much we love you." Cut each sheet of paper lengthwise into three, then into five across for fifteen notes per sheet. Copy centers sell individual sheets of parchment and other decorative paper for about $.75 each.

150 packets of seeds	$225.00
Ten sheets of 8½″ × 14″ parchment paper	7.50
Total	$232.50

(This will make 150 favors @ $1.55 each.)

Instant Photo Favors

As each single guest or couple arrives at the reception, take their picture using a Polaroid or other instant camera; then, attach each photo to a large silk ficus tree at the reception, along with a loving note from the bride and groom thanking the guests for sharing the day. As the guests leave, ask them to search the tree for their photos, which they may keep as favors.

Polaroid or other instant camera film ($.55 per photo)	$82.50
Ten sheets of 8½″ × 14″ parchment paper	7.50
Total	$90.00

(This will make 150 favors @ $.60 each.)

Personal Message Rolled Into a Scroll

This is the idea our daughter and son-in-law used. They wrote a personal message, thanking the guests for sharing the day with them, etc. Then they had this message copied onto a "master" by a calligrapher. This was duplicated nine times onto a legal-sized sheet of plain white paper. This sheet was then used as the "master" to be copied onto twenty-three pieces of parchment paper. It required that much parchment cut into nine "scrolls" each, to give them 207 scrolls. (One was given to each single person or couple.) Each of the scrolls was rolled up and tied with a narrow ribbon and two small gold rings.

Twenty-three pieces of 8½″ × 14″ parchment paper	$17.25
Twenty-three copies on copy machine	2.30
Ribbon	9.00
Gold-colored rings	7.00
Total	$35.55

(This will make 207 favors @ $.17 each.)

Wedding Couple Bubble Bottles

Each individual guest is given a wedding couple bubble bottle, tied at the neck with ribbon. As the bride and groom make their getaway at the end of the reception, the guests line the walkway to the getaway vehicle and blow bubbles over the heads of the couple. These bubble bottles are available in craft and wedding supply stores everywhere, but the least expensive I could find were through Oriental Trading Company (see Resources on pages 176-179) at twenty-four bottles for $3.95.

Bubble bottles ($.17 per bottle)	$34.00
Ribbon	$9.00
Total	$43.00

(This will make 200 favors @ $.22 each.)

Krispy Kreme Doughnuts

As this Edition goes to press, there is a new gimmicky trend developing in wedding favors: furnishing each guest a fresh Krispy Kreme donut as he or she leaves the reception. Of course, Krispy Kreme donuts are extremely popular throughout the country in general, but the idea of giving them away as "wedding favors" is quite the thing. Some brides are even foregoing a traditional wedding cake in favor of these melt-in-the-mouth treats which are fashioned into a unique cake, using about 150 donuts. One bride had a Krispy Kreme truck drive up with fresh donuts for each guest as she and her groom were leaving in a limo. If you like this idea, the donuts will run about $6.50 per dozen, including tax, depending on where you live. That's about $.54 per guest.

Seventeen dozen donuts ($.54 per donut)	$110.16
Total	$110.16

(This will provide 200 "favors" @ $.54 each.)

Last-Minute Alterations
Approximate Cost *$75*

There may be a few unexpected glitches in the way everything fits, from bridesmaids' dresses to the wedding gown. People sometimes lose or gain weight close to the wedding.

It will usually save you quite a bit of money if you forego the seamstress at the bridal salon and provide for your own alterations; some bridal salons charge as much as $250 to alter a wedding gown.

Guest Book and Pen
Approximate Cost *$18*

You can purchase a fancy set for up to $50 or you can buy a plain book with "Guests" printed on the cover, the type intended to be used in your home. The inside pages are the same. Use a plain white ball-point pen tied with a ribbon.

Guest Book Alternatives
Parchment Scroll. *$1*

Modern brides have come up with some other interesting alternatives to the standard wedding guest book, as well: one idea is to provide a 19″ × 25″ piece of off-white parchment paper that you roll into a tight scroll and then let unwind, creating a lovely document for your guests to sign. After the wedding, this scroll may be kept as a memento by framing it or re-rolling it and tying with a ribbon.

Wedding Guest Artwork *$40*

Another trendy idea is to provide sheets of paper, along with crayons and felt-tip markers (one set per table) for the guests to write messages or draw pictures—a truly clever alternative to the traditional guest book.

Engagement Photo With Extra-Wide Matting *$20*

Have your guests sign a wide white matting around your engagement photo, as it stands on a floor easel at eye level at the reception. (The $20 covers the cost of the matting and doesn't include the cost of the photo.)

Kneeling Bench or Cushion
Approximate Cost *$15*

If a kneeling bench is required for your ceremony, borrow one from the church itself. If they don't have one, rent one from a florist or wedding rental store. Rental benches run from $5 to $20.

Table Skirts
Approximate Cost . . . . *3 × $10 ea. = $30*

You'll probably be able to borrow the table linen for the reception, but most people don't own table skirts. The disposable variety are fine and only cost about $10 each.

Sheet Music for Musicians
Approximate Cost *$15*

A church organist and the other musicians will almost always have the music you need for your wedding. However, you may need to buy at least one piece of music that no one seems to have. In our case, we purchased the sheet music for the "Wedding March" from *The Sound of Music* for the organist to play as the recessional.

Ring Bearer's Pillow
Approximate Cost *$15*

Although you can spruce up an old Easter basket for the flower girl, the ring bearer does need a clean, white satin pillow. If you can borrow or make one, you can save the money; otherwise, watch for a sale.

Garters for the Bride
Approximate Cost *$10*

You'll need two garters: one to keep and one to toss. In our daughter's case, the one she kept was the one I wore when I was married. Sometimes garters are available in sets of two for $7 or $8.

Grand total of probable miscellaneous expenses: $878.00

Ouch! That stings, doesn't it? I told you these annoying expenses are like a swarm of yellow jackets; at least you've been warned and won't be unpleasantly surprised later. These costs are usually ignored because the bride's family is so concerned about the wedding gown, the cake, the flowers and all the other seemingly larger expenses. And because these expenses don't seem to fit into a category, they go off by themselves and multiply like rabbits in the summertime. Well, in the next chapter these expenses are added into the totals, so you will cross your finish line without pain.

Extra Expenses You Can Probably Do Without:

Luggage for the Honeymoon
If you don't already have enough pieces for your trip, borrow them.

Aisle Runner
Do without it! Even most White House weddings do without an aisle runner because the wedding gown photographs better against a darker color. We didn't have a runner for our daughter's wedding, and the dark blue carpet really set off her gown. Also, if the aisle runner is very white, it can make an off-white wedding gown look dirty.

Going-Away Outfit

Wear something you already have. Also, it has become popular to go on the "wedding parade" in the full wedding attire and then change into very casual clothes before leaving on the honeymoon. Some brides and grooms even wear jeans.

Makeup Artist

"Facial artistry," as it is called, has become a "must" lately. There are professionals who will come in for an hourly rate and make up the entire wedding party. Instead, have the bridesmaids make each other up, and have the maid or matron of honor assist the bride. You can get free make-over ideas beforehand by having a professional apply your makeup at a finer department store cosmetic department. The important thing to remember is to take it easy on the makeup—don't overdo it to the point where the bride doesn't even look like herself, which often happens when an amateur goes crazy.

> *Tip* I've received several letters from my readers who said they made arrangements with their Mary Kay consultants to provide a professional makeup makeover for the bride and her attendants on the morning of the wedding.

Hair Appointments

Unless your hair is very difficult to manage, have a friend or another family member help you with it.

Manicures

In the same way, do each others' nails. They will be beautiful!

Groom's Cake

A groom's cake is very popular in the South, but often omitted at weddings elsewhere around the country. It's almost always a dark fruitcake, but it can also be dark chocolate. It can be cut up in tiny squares and placed in little white boxes with the bride and groom's initials or it can just be served on a separate table from the bride's cake for those who prefer a different flavor. If you have a loving grandma who would love to bake fruitcakes for the occasion, that would be very nice, but it certainly isn't a necessary expense.

Nursery

Some etiquette books say a wedding is no place for small children; however, most daytime weddings I've attended seem to have plenty of them running around. That is why an attended nursery can be a delightful convenience for the parents, including the wedding party who may have small children. We provided paid nursery workers for our daughter's wedding, but it certainly is not an expected service. Our cost was $45 total for the wedding rehearsal and ceremony only. During the reception, the parents were on their own.

Bride and Groom's Engraved Champagne Glasses
Borrow the most beautiful glasses you can find; just tie each with white satin ribbon. If you decide to buy a set, they run about $18 at a wedding supply store.

Cake Server
Borrow a nice silver one from a friend or relative; tie with white satin ribbon. If you decide to buy one, it will run about $30.

Programs for the Ceremony
Programs are nice to have because they identify the members of the wedding party. They also give the order of the ceremony so the guests can follow along. You can make up a good computer master that you can copy and fold yourself for a total of about $25. Otherwise, forget them. Only about half the weddings I attend furnish them anyway.

Lighting Technician
If the church or synagogue's lighting system is complex, the church may offer the services of their lighting person who will assist for a nominal fee. Otherwise, see if you can find a talented friend to help. In our case, the available lighting was no problem; we just turned it on and adjusted it before the service and no extra help was needed.

Clergyman's Fee
This fee is the responsibility of the groom and will vary from $50 to $400. By the way, there is an interesting trend developing: some states will ordain a friend or relative for the day for a reasonable fee.

Wedding Insurance
Wedding insurance costs about $250 and covers such things as reimbursing nonrefundable deposits in case the wedding is canceled or postponed due to a natural disaster or death/illness of a family member or member of the bridal party. The bulk of the coverage, however, is for property damage, which is a rare occurrence. I feel that unless a family member is gravely ill and there is a possibility the person may pass away close to the wedding date, wedding insurance isn't a necessity. First of all, most vendors will work with you on the deposits, especially if the wedding is only being postponed. In the case of a member of the wedding party becoming ill or passing away quite suddenly, the wedding can usually go on as planned with another person filling in. The decision is up to you, but this is definitely an expense you can forego.

Calligrapher

Some brides hire a calligrapher to address all the invitations, reply envelopes, and thank-you notes. A calligrapher charges by the hour and it takes many hours to complete this task. In my daughter's case, we bought the proper type of black calligraphy pen and I did them myself. I took it nice and slow and used a few extra "loops" and "twirls." Some people thought we had them done professionally, but actually anyone with decent handwriting can do a lovely job if they have the right pen and plenty of time.

Lodging for Out-of-Town Guests and/or Wedding Party

This expense is usually paid by the guests or members of the wedding party. If the bride's family feels, however, that this would be a burdensome expense, they can make other arrangements. One suggestion is to ask friends and other family members to "put them up."

Linen Tablecloths, Punch Bowls, Serving Plates, etc.

If the reception is held in a social hall connected to the church or synagogue, everything you need should be included in the rental fee for the site. If you must provide anything yourself, borrow like crazy. There are white linen tablecloths sitting in drawers all over town, as well as punch bowls of all sizes and lovely serving platters and bowls. After a couple of phone calls, you'll have everything you need and more.

Last-Minute Pressing of Bridesmaids' Dresses or Other Attire

We brought three dresses to the dry cleaners at the last minute to have them "touched up." One had been in a suitcase and the other two had never been pressed out when purchased. We paid $6 to have one pressed and $9 each for two bridesmaids' dresses. This was more for convenience than anything. To save these costs, just keep your ironing board up, use a good press cloth, and do it yourself.

11

Second Weddings

(Trends and Cost-Cutting Tips for Second-Time Brides)

If you're a second-time bride, this chapter is especially for you. Although a second wedding can be a full-blown affair, with traditional, floor-length gown, seven bridal attendants and five hundred guests, the trend is toward a smaller wedding with less-elaborate bridal attire, fewer bridesmaids and fewer guests. In fact, according to a recent survey conducted by *Bride Again* magazine, the total cost of 71 percent of second and third weddings average less than $12,999. I've also discovered from interviews I've conducted with second-wedding brides and grooms, that they have discovered "less" is often "more" when it comes to planning a deeply poignant, personalized, meaningful wedding.

Many second-time brides I've spoken with seem to feel they've "been there—done that" with their first weddings. If your first marriage ended in divorce, you've undoubtedly suffered through a lot of heartache, and because of what you've been through, you may prefer a less-elaborate wedding this time, one where the emphasis is on the sanctity of the vows and the sacred quality of the ceremony. On the other hand, if you were happily married and lost your spouse through death, you've also suffered a great deal and may want to plan an intimate family wedding, especially if your first wedding was large and extravagant. In fact, most of the widows I've spoken with want to avoid anything that reminds them of their first wedding, from the wedding gown to the flowers to the reception theme.

Second-time grooms have interesting perspectives, as well. Instead of spending the big bucks on the wedding, they prefer to spend more on the honeymoon. In fact, many of the second-time grooms I've spoken with like the idea of bypassing the big hometown wedding altogether, preferring a simple, yet meaningful, ceremony at their honeymoon destination. This type of wedding, by the way, is also called a *honeymoon wedding, travel wedding,* or *destination wedding.* In my book, *Picture-Perfect, Worry-Free Weddings: 72 Destinations and Venues,* I describe the various types of destination wedding options, many of which are quite affordable, including these destinations: Walt Disney World; Lake Tahoe, Nevada; Las Vegas, Nevada; the Poconos in Pennsylvania; Pigeon Forge, Tennessee; national parks; the Caribbean; cruise ships; Hawaii; Fiji and Mexico.

If the idea of a honeymoon wedding sounds good to you, you may want to pick up a copy of my book to read more about these various destinations, along with real-life stories of couples who chose this option.

Other popular options for a second wedding are the *K.I.S.S. wedding* (keep it sweet and simple), the *surprise wedding* and a *combination wedding*. *Picture-Perfect, Worry-Free Weddings* also includes details for these affordable weddings. For example, a K.I.S.S. wedding may be a simple Beach Party Wedding, a Denim Required Wedding, Patio Party Wedding, Picnic-in-the-Park Wedding or a fun-for-everyone Houseboat Wedding. A surprise or combination wedding may take place during any number of get-togethers, including a Valentine's party, New Year's Eve party, engagement celebration, singles' club meeting, Toastmasters' Club meeting or during a family function, such as Thanksgiving, Christmas, Fourth of July or a family reunion.

If you have your heart set on a traditional wedding, however, just scaled down a little, here are second-wedding trends to consider:

Affordable Wedding Venues

- Small chapel

- Bed and breakfast

- Private home or garden

- Historical site, such as a mansion, lighthouse or a restored Victorian home

- Public venues, such as a rose garden or a lakeside setting

Bride's Attire

- Tea-length or street-length cocktail dress

- Dressy suit

- A flattering dress from the Fine Dresses section of your department store

- Bridesmaid's gown in off-white or pastel shade

- Rent a wedding gown

Groom's Attire
- Dark suit

- Dark blue blazer and white or beige slacks

Attendants
- One bridal attendant (maid or matron of honor)

- One groomsman (best man)

- Children from previous marriage included in the wedding party, as bridesmaids, flower girl, groomsmen or ring bearer

Flowers
- Fewer arrangements

- Less-elaborate arrangements, bouquets, boutonnieres and corsages

- Basic supermarket floral department wedding package

Music
- One instrumentalist, such as a guitarist, harpist or pianist

- One soloist, for the ceremony only

- Taped music or an amateur or professional DJ for the reception

Decorations
- Smaller venues call for fewer decorations

- Keep it simple with no pew bows, borrowed white lace tablecloths for the reception, a few candles, plus affordable helium-filled balloons at the reception site

Reception Food
- Mid-afternoon cake, coffee and champagne only

- Mid-morning breakfast buffet

- Evening dessert-only reception

- Light finger-food luncheon buffet

❦ Affordable wedding cake options (see chapter six for great money-saving ideas)

Photography and Videography

❦ Enlist the help of amateur photographers and videographers (see chapter nine for helpful tips)

❦ Basic professional photography or videography packages

Miscellaneous Expenses

❦ Eliminate the aisle runner, makeup artist, hair stylist, manicurist, groom's cake, ceremony programs, reception favors and bride's garter

❦ Instead of stretch limousines, rent or borrow town cars, Cadillacs or classic cars

Another touching trend with second weddings is toward personalized vows. In my book, *Diane Warner's Complete Book of Wedding Vows* (Career Press), I include these special chapters: "Vows for Second Marriages" and "Vows for Older Couples." All of the vows in these two chapters are nontraditional, personalized vows, geared toward the second-time bride and groom, their children, and older couples, many of whom became widowed later in their first marriages. Here I've included a few vows from the book.

For a second-time bride and groom:

"_____, you are my healer, my comforter, and the joy of my life. Your love has restored my torn, broken heart; your smile has healed my pain; and your caring spirit has rescued mine from the dark places. I love you _____, and I vow to be a faithful, loving husband/wife, to care for you, to comfort you and to cherish you for as long as we both shall live."

For an older couple:

"Because of you, I'm no longer lonely; because of you, my life is brand new; because of you, my heart is singing—no more sorrows, no more tears. Because of you, my days are filled with hope and excitement, just to be with you, letting your love soak into my dry bones until they are strong and filled with your energy. I am young again, dear _____, all because of you. I need you now and always, every waking moment, and I freely and wholly give myself to you this day, to be your loving and faithful husband/wife, and to be true to you always, as long as the Lord gives us together in this life."

The personalized vows popular today are shared not only between the bride and groom, but include their children, as well. Sixty-four percent of second wedding couples have children from previous marriages, so it's not surprising the children are becoming an important part of the ceremony. The vows that include children are especially heart-tugging, including a vow from the groom to his soon-to-be-step-daughter that includes placing a ring on her finger.

Depending on the ages of your children, you may want them to walk you down the aisle, read a poem or a few verses of scripture, perform a musical selection; or you may decide to include your children in the unity candle celebration (where the bride, groom and their children each hold lighted candles that are used to light a single larger candle, signifying the unifying of two families into one).

A vow that includes the bride's daughter from a previous marriage (grab a tissue for this one!):

> "_____, I love your Mommy, and today I have taken her as my wife; but did you know that I love you dearly as well? I want to be as a father to you, and I invite you into my heart. We will have happy times together, you and your Mommy and I. And with this ring I give you my love." (He slides a ring onto the girl's finger.)

These are only three of the vow segments found in my book, which contains 185 pages filled with more touching, poignant personalized vows for second weddings.

If you adopt only a few of the cost-saving second-wedding trends, you'll probably save enough money for an extra-special honeymoon. And if you place the emphasis on the sanctity of the ceremony, personalized vows, and including your children in the ceremony and reception, you'll have a very special wedding day.

As you consider all your options, you'll also benefit by taking a good look back at your first wedding and asking yourself these questions:

❧ What was the biggest waste of money?

❧ What was really worth the money?

❧ What was missing from my first wedding that I want included this time?

As I end this chapter on second weddings, I want to leave you with a few encouraging words. Second and third weddings no longer have stigmas attached; they can be as creative as can be—whatever your heart's desire! So, go for it!

Forget the outdated rules of etiquette that restrict the color and style of your wedding gown—if you want to wear a traditional white gown, enjoy it to the hilt! On the other hand, if you decide to get married at the top of a ski slope, or on the shore of your favorite water skiing lake, do it!

It's your wedding and you deserve one that will bring you joy and hope for a happy future together.

12

Tips for Your Groom
(Money-Saving Ideas for the Man in Your Life)

I assume your fiancée has handed this book over to you so you can save some money, too. Am I right? Because over 70 percent of brides and grooms are paying for the entire wedding themselves, chances are that your savings are quickly being depleted. Even if you aren't sharing in the cost of the wedding itself, you're undoubtedly being saddled with these incidental expenses already discussed in previous chapters:

- ❦ Your share of the florist's bill

- ❦ The clergyman's fee

- ❦ Your blood test and the marriage license

- ❦ The rental or purchase of your wedding attire

In addition to these expected expenses, you have five more that are yours exclusively:

- ❦ Bride's Engagement Ring

- ❦ Wedding Bands

- ❦ The Getaway Vehicle

- ❦ A Gift For Your Bride

- ❦ The Honeymoon

I have some brilliant suggestions for each of these items—not all of which are my brain children for, I must admit, I have interviewed hundreds of grooms who have agreed to share their money-saving ideas with you.

First of all, let's talk about wedding jewelry and the best ways to have high quality on a small budget.

Bride's Engagement Ring

I don't know if you've already shopped for her ring, but if you've been window-shopping in retail jewelry store windows, you're probably still pale from the sticker-shock! First of all, the worst place to go shopping is your retail jewelry store, unless they're having a whopping-good sale. Here are some smart alternatives:

Family Heirloom Ring
No Cost $0

If you're lucky, there may be a lovely heirloom ring rattling around a dresser drawer somewhere in your family; it may be an antique setting passed down from your great-grandmother, or an exquisite dinner ring sitting in a safety-deposit box, leftover from your great-aunt's estate. Give this idea some serious thought because an heirloom ring may be the most poignant, touching gift you can give her. (This is a popular alternative these days, by the way.)

Set an Existing Diamond
Approximate Cost . . . . $75–$175

If you've been given an heirloom ring, but the setting is inappropriate, you can have the existing diamond(s) lifted out of the antique ring and placed in a new setting. In one case, a man was given his grandfather's Masonic ring which had a black onyx base on top of a heavy gold band with a large center diamond; he took the ring to the jeweler's and had the gold in the band melted down into a modern Tiffany setting and the single diamond lifted and set to create a stunning solitaire engagement ring.

There are other sources of used diamonds, as well, such as estate sales, pawn shops and classified ads. However, these are risky places to shop for a diamond and I don't recommend them because it's usually impossible to verify the diamond's authenticity before making the purchase; if you have a knowledgeable friend who will accompany you, or if you're allowed to bring the diamond or piece of jewelry to a professional appraiser before committing yourself, this may be a possibility.

Set a Temporary Synthetic Diamond
Approximate Cost $100

Here's an idea that is gaining popularity, but it's only a possibility if your bride goes along with the idea. For the time being, purchase a synthetic diamond which is the same size as the authentic diamond you plan to replace it with at a later date. Surprisingly, this clever idea was revealed to me in confidence by several retail jewelers who told me how popular this trick has become, and every one of them admitted that, unless someone has a trained eye, a good quality synthetic diamond looks enough like the real thing to "fool the girls at the office," at least until the groom can afford to replace it with the genuine article when his finances straighten out after the honeymoon.

If you decide to pursue this idea, however, be sure your bride approves of this clandestine plan, and, most important: Don't share this beautifully devious news with anyone! It will be your own little secret—just between you and your bride. Then, on a later date—perhaps as a Christmas or birthday gift, or on your first anniversary—you'll have the joy of presenting her with the diamond of her choice.

Give an Engagement Ring With a Birthstone Instead of a Diamond
Approximate Cost . . . . **$100–$500**

An engagement ring doesn't have to be set with a diamond to be "official"; there are many other stones that are quite beautiful, as well, including aquamarine, pearl, opal and amethyst.

Buy It Wholesale for 50 Percent Off Retail Price

By shopping around you can find ways to purchase a new ring of your choice without having to pay full retail price. One of the best sources is your wholesale diamond broker, often accessible only when accompanied by someone with a seller's resale permit, although many are also open to the public. The good news is when you purchase a diamond ring from one of these brokers, you'll usually save at least 50 percent off retail. The bad news is that you'll have to pay cash on the spot.

Other ways to save 50 percent off retail is to purchase through a discount catalog store or though a retailer who may be having a special limited-time 50 percent off retail sale, often during the two-week period preceding Valentine's Day.

Just remember that by shopping around you can find a diamond your fiancée will love at a discount of 50 percent, or more, off the suggested retail price.

Warning: Become Fluent in the "Four Cs"

Regardless of where you plan to shop for your bride's diamond, you need to be educated in the Four Cs:

❧ **Clarity**
Clarity is ranked on a scale from *F1* (flawless) to *F13* (imperfect); the differences in clarity are said to be difficult to discern with the naked eye. An *F1* diamond can run from $1,000 to $5,000 more than a comparable diamond with an *F13* ranking.

❧ **Color**
Color refers to the color of the diamond itself, which ranges from

D (colorless) to *Y* (yellow). This quality is more discernible to the naked eye, but usually only when diamonds are compared side by side in strong sunlight. The price differences between a *D* and a *Y* ranking are similar to those for clarity; a *D* being the higher priced.

❦ *Carat*

Carat indicates the weight of the diamond; a one-carat diamond, for example, weighs twice as much and is twice the size of a half-carat diamond. The carat weight is obviously the most discernible quality to the naked eye. The average carat weight of an engagement ring diamond in the United States today, by the way, is .75; this is according to a survey published in *USA Today.*

❦ *Cut*

The cut of the diamond refers to its shape and number of facets; the general shape of the diamond is easy to see, but the number of facets are not as obvious. The more facets, the more brilliance as you turn the diamond back and forth under a strong light.

My own little personal survey, by the way, shows that most women prefer a larger diamond that has a few "invisible" flaws over a smaller one that is closer to perfect.

When you go shopping for a diamond, a one-carat, colorless, flawless marquise cut will probably be the first you'll be shown by the jeweler, who hopes to sell you one of his more expensive pieces. Be prepared to be hit with the "two-months' salary" rule, as well, which is a rule of thumb, conveniently calculated by jewelers and diamond merchants who want you to spend two months' of your salary on the ring. Remember that this is *their* idea, not yours, and you should spend no more than is comfortable for you. Don't forget that you can always add a more expensive setting or an extra diamond or two some day when your income is higher and you don't have so many other wedding and honeymoon expenses to pay for all at once.

Wedding Bands

Create Wedding Bands From Used Gold
Approximate Cost . . . . **$100–$200**

Used gold is much easier to round up than a used diamond, and many couples are having their wedding bands poured from old, removed gold fillings or dental bridgework or from existing gold jewelry, whether antique or not. One groom I know brought a gold bridge and a couple gold caps to his jeweler, along with an old gold ring that had been in his family, hoping the total weight would be enough to create a "chunky" wedding band for himself. The result was that the dental gold alone was more than enough for a large band that would have retailed for over $800; his total cost, however, was only $125. The family ring contained enough gold to pour a wedding band for his bride, as well, for an additional cost of only $100. So, you see? If you have any gold dental work replaced, be sure to take it home with you, and do some "constructive snooping" among your family members to see if anyone has an old gold chain in need of repair, a bracelet, ring or pin which could be melted down and poured into the mold of your choice. Brilliant idea!

Wedding Bands at 50 Percent Off Retail Price
Approximate Cost . . . . *$75–$150*

Shop for your bands from the same discount sources mentioned earlier: wholesale jewelry brokers; discount catalog stores or through a retail jewelry store that's having a sale.

The Getaway Vehicle

It's a trend these days to hire one limousine to serve triple-duty:

1. Transporting the wedding party to the ceremony site

2. Transporting the bride and groom from the ceremony to the reception

3. As a getaway vehicle for the bride and groom

This is fine and good except that limousines don't come cheap, averaging approximately $100 each per hour, plus tips. Frankly, they have become just a little boring, wouldn't you say? After all, you can't even see through the darkened glass, so they're no fun at all for the guests!

Here are some interesting, affordable alternatives that you might want to consider, depending on where you live and who you know:

❧ *Borrow or Rent a Cadillac or Lincoln Town Car*
Know any affluent friends or relatives who might loan you their luxury vehicle for the day? Or, do as one couple did—rent a Town Car for $50 for twenty-four hours, which certainly beats the cost of a limo!

❧ *Any Convertible*
Tie on the balloons and streamers and sit on top of the back seat as you leave the reception. A convertible works especially well because there's plenty of room for the bride's gown and veil.

❧ *A Decorated Jeep*
One couple I know decorated an old rusty Jeep, wrapping it in white crepe paper and decorating it with paper flowers, streamers and

balloons and then "skirting" it with disposable, white plastic ruffled table skirting. The wedding party had fun decorating it and when they were finished they had an elegant "float" for showing off the bride and groom on the ride through town.

❧ A Decorated Pickup Truck

The same idea works for a pickup truck by "skirting" and "ballooning" the bed where the bride and groom sit on decorated lawn chairs for the wedding parade following the reception.

❧ Hay Wagon

How about an old-fashioned hay ride? In one case the entire wedding party piled aboard the hay bales, escorted the bride and groom to the airport and then continued on their way, not wanting the party to end. It's great if you have a farmer or rancher in the family, otherwise, any flatbed truck or trailer will do. If you have to rent, the rental plus the bales of hay will run about $300.

❧ A Snowmobile or Horse-Drawn Sleigh

If you're marrying in the winter and there's plenty of snow on the ground, you might want to consider one of these fun alternatives. A horse and sleigh rig will rent for $150 to $600 for the day.

❧ A Classic or Antique Car

If you know anyone who has a cute old car, whether a Model T or '55 Chevy, ask if you can borrow or rent it for the wedding. A good source is your local classic car club where the members are so "into" their vehicles you may even find one who will offer to serve as your driver, just for a chance to personally show off his toy.

❧ Up, Up and Away

You may be one of those lucky people who just happens to know a hot air balloonist or someone who has access to a helicopter. Wouldn't that make a dramatic statement as you "lift off"?

❧ Novelty Getaways

You can really wow them by galloping off on horseback (be sure to braid the horses' tails and manes with white satin ribbons!), chugging away on a little red tractor, peddling off on a decorated bicycle-built-for-two, or, how about a little yellow school bus?

The important thing is to look for a novel, affordable alternative to the standard limo. You might even come up with an idea that won't cost you a penny, except for the fuel. And here's an extra tip: if your vehicle requires a driver, rent him his own top hat!

Note: If your wedding requires several vehicles to transport a large number, go with the trend: rent a party bus instead. They are usually available through a limousine rental company, but less expensive than renting several limos. Many party buses come fully equipped with comfortable chairs, sound system, and a restroom. Or you can create your own "party bus" by decorating someone's mini-van or RV for the day.

A Gift for Your Bride

The bride and groom usually talk over their gift-giving ideas so that they're on the same page when it comes to buying gifts for each other and, in fact, many couples decide to forego these gifts and put their money toward the wedding or their honeymoon. On the other hand, it's very special to give your bride a personal gift, something she'll treasure always—a gift from her husband on her wedding day! And it's usually a good idea for this gift to be something lasting, something your bride can touch, hold or wear throughout her married life.

Here are some affordable, yet meaningful, choices:

Cultured Pearl Necklace or Earrings
Approximate Cost . . . . *$40–$250*

Depending on whether you choose a single pearl on a gold chain, a strand of pearls or a pair of pearl earrings, your gift will be quite affordable if you shop the discount market, as I have already described. Note: there are simulated pearls and cultured pearls, and it is the latter which is considered suitable as a wedding gift.

Diamond Drop Necklace or Earrings
Approximate Cost . . . . *$130–$500*

Diamonds are obviously more expensive than pearls, but again, if you shop the discount market, you'll find a stunning gift within this price range.

14K Gold Heart Pendant or Locket
Approximate Cost . . . . *Under $150*

You can find a beautifully engraved heart-shaped pendant or locket on a gold chain for less than $150, again by shopping the discount market.

Precious Moments Figurine
Approximate Cost . . . . *$50–$90*

Here's a sweet, poignant gift idea, especially if your bride happens to be a fan of Precious Moments. Within this price range you can purchase one of these figurines, entitled "I Give You My Love Forever True," a bride and groom with flowers at their feet that stands about six and a half inches high. Another, entitled "Sealed With a Kiss," is a bisque figurine of a bride and groom kissing over the mailbox of their new home and stands about five and a half inches high. All Precious Moments figurines are collectibles that should appreciate in value every year; they can be purchased at most fine gift shops.

Music Box
Approximate Cost . . . . ***$30–$150***

If you're the sentimental type and you really want to wow your bride with a "warm, fuzzy" gift, how about a music box? Most women love music boxes. These lovely, yet affordable, gifts can be purchased at many Hallmark stores, department stores, gift shops, The San Francisco Music Box Company (often found in shopping malls), or through a discount catalog store. One of my favorite music boxes has an open porcelain book with a love poem written on one page, two love doves perched on the other, and plays the song "Wind Beneath My Wings."

Book of Love Poems
Approximate Cost . . . . ***$6–$40***

Don't let the frugality of this gift fool you—any bride would love to receive a book of love poems from her groom, especially if he writes something endearing on the dedication page. A popular choice is a book by Elizabeth Barrett Browning entitled *Sonnets from the Portuguese.* Or, if you're a poet, write her something truly original to express your love for her and your feelings about your wedding day. For only six dollars you can purchase a "blank book," a beautifully bound book that has empty pages, all ready and waiting for your original verse (or, you can cheat a little and steal a phrase or two from some of those mushy love cards at Hallmark!).

The Honeymoon

Ah, finally we come to your biggest expense of all—the honeymoon! If you're like most grooms-to-be, you're probably wondering how there will ever be enough money left over for that wonderfully romantic honeymoon you have in mind. Well, I sympathize with you, but take a big breath and read on, for there *is* hope—I guarantee it!

According to a recent *Bride's* magazine poll, the average cost of a honeymoon is $3,200. Assuming your bank account is down to $1,500, or $1,000, or even less, here are your best honeymoon buys, categorized by price range.

Free Honeymoons
A free honeymoon! Is there such a thing? You bet there is, and here's how you can have it:

Honeymoon Gift Registry

Establish a gift registry at your favorite travel agency, in the same way you would establish a registry at a department store or gift shop. Spread the word, cross your fingers, and hope that enough comes in to pay for your *entire* honeymoon! If your only registry is through a travel agency, you're more likely to have enough.

Hideaway Honeymoon at Home

This is one of the brilliant ideas I discovered when I was a contributing editor for *Honeymoon* magazine. I had no idea so many couples were doing this! Here's the drill:

1. Tell everyone you're flying to the Bahamas (or somewhere) for your honeymoon.

2. Don't tell *anyone* you're actually honeymooning in your own home or apartment—not *even* your parents or best man!

3. A few days before the wedding, stock your "secret honeymoon nest" with goodies: prepared foods from the deli; plenty of things to drink including, of course, champagne; paper plates, cups, plastic champagne glasses; candles (lots and lots of candles!); romantic CDs and tapes; bubble bath; massage oil; an ample supply of sheets and towels; fresh strawberries; several boxes of chocolates; your favorite cologne and perfume; and a couple dozen movies on video or DVD (not that you'll really watch them all, of course).

4. Bring packed suitcases with you to the reception that can be placed (in full view of your guests) in the trunk of your getaway vehicle to convince everyone you're really flying off somewhere!

5. Be sure you aren't followed home after the reception. If necessary, head for the airport and stay on that route until you've ditched the last of the wedding party who may be following you.

6. Once you're home, hide your car in the garage, unplug the telephone and don't answer the door—no matter what!

Isn't this a deliciously devious idea? Of course, in a year or so you'll be able to afford that exotic honeymoon you originally had in mind, and you'll appreciate it all the more by then.

Honeymoons Less Than $1,000

Believe it or not, there are actually quite a few honeymoons that fit this category:

❧ *Take a Short Cruise*

Depending on where you live and how easy it is for you to get to the point of embarkation, there are honeymoon cruises available for about $500 per person, all-inclusive. Several embark from Florida and others from Los Angeles and San Diego.

❦ *Escape to the Poconos!*

The Pocono Honeymoon Resorts, located in the Pocono Mountains of Pennsylvania, absolutely drip with sensuality, with their deep, heart-shaped whirlpool tubs, private swimming pools, velvet-draped canopied beds, candlelit dinners, free entertainment and recreational opportunities. It's no wonder their all-inclusive packages are such honeymoon favorites. Call 1-800-POCONOS for free brochures.

❦ *Rent a Private Residence, Cabin or Condo*

Contact the Visitor's Bureau at your honeymoon destination and ask for a list of rental agencies who offer private rentals. Even Lake Tahoe, which is a picture perfect honeymoon setting, has offerings starting at about $400 per week. Then, of course, you'll need to do a little cooking, or bring in deli or take-out foods, which should leave money left over for a couple of splurges.

❦ *Nightlife-Wilderness Combo*

You can enjoy the nightlife of Las Vegas, which is actually quite affordable if you take advantage of the free entertainment, all-you-can-eat buffets and nearby "nature escapes" to the Black Canyon.

❦ *Borrow or Rent an RV or a Houseboat*

What could be more romantic than the sound of raindrops pinging against the metal roof of your RV or houseboat as you cuddle in a sleeping bag made for two, or the smell of bacon frying over an open campfire alongside a secluded lake in a national park, or a walk in the moonlight along a deserted beach? Give it some thought—you may even have a friend or relative who would loan you a cozy unit, cutting your cost even further.

❦ *A Long-Weekend Honeymoon*

Stay at picturesque, but affordable, spots in your home state that include at least one meal in the price, such as a bed-and-breakfast; then go everywhere and do everything that's "fun but cheap": sightseeing and people-watching; attending free festivals and concerts; poking around a flea market; free-loading dinner off a "happy hour buffet" for the price of a couple of drinks; lunching with a picnic basket full of romantic goodies at the beach or a scenic overlook. When a couple is in love, it's amazing how fun and wonderful and romantic everything seems to be, because, as we all know, it's *who you're with* that really counts!

Honeymoons Less Than $1,500

❦ Take a Longer Cruise

Call any discount cruise company of your choice, such as Cruise Line, Inc. If you can afford $1,500 for your honeymoon, there are several romantic cruises available at about $750 per person.

❦ Fly or Drive to Mexico or Canada

Our neighbors to the north and south offer some very affordable stays, depending on how close you live to one of their borders. Sun-Trips, Delta Dream Vacations and American Airlines Vacations offer some of the best packages to cities in Mexico, including Cancun, Puerto Vallarta, Mazatlan, Los Cabos, Mexico City and Guadalajara.

Canada is an easy destination if you live anywhere near its border. If you're in the northwest, visit Vancouver, Victoria and the San Juan Islands or cross over to Prince Albert in Saskatchewan and visit the Prince Albert National Park; or visit Winnipeg in Manitoba which offers many scenic walking tours and people-watching opportunities; or, the city of Quebec will give you the feeling of being in Paris.

❦ An Adventure Honeymoon

You can stay well within the $1,500 range by planning a sporting or adventure honeymoon. You may want to charter a boat for a deep-sea-fishing trip, or sign up for a golfer's package or reserve a week at a dude ranch or guest ranch. (Word of caution: Look for one that is "adults-only.") If the fishing idea sounds good, go to your local magazine stand and purchase several of the most popular fishing magazines, including *Sport Fishing, Field and Stream* or *Outdoor Life*, where you'll find ads for various package trips. If you're a golfer, of course, look for ads in *Golf* or *Golf Digest*, and if the dude ranch idea is appealing, go to your library or purchase Gene Kilgore's book entitled *Ranch Vacations*.

The important thing to remember is that the success of your honeymoon doesn't depend on how much you spend, but the fact that you can be together, uninterrupted, after the stress and hoopla of the wedding plans and your wedding day itself. Any setting is a romantic setting, after all, when you only have eyes for each other and are relishing your new roles as husband and wife.

Cost-Cutting Tips While You're on Your Honeymoon

Meanwhile, no matter where you spend your honeymoon, here are some general common-sense cost-cutting tips:

❧ Be sure to pack plenty of film, toothpaste, shampoo and suntan lotion, the four things most likely to need replacing at your honeymoon site where they will cost more than at your hometown discount drug store.

❧ Don't even think of touching your hotel room's mini-bar.

❧ Don't phone home—too expensive, especially if from your hotel room where they may tack on a per-call service charge. If you must call home, purchase a calling card ahead of time at a reasonable per/minute rate.

❧ Always take advantage of the complimentary breakfasts offered by your hotel; even if it's only continental, it may at least pacify you until lunch.

❧ Consider picking up an *Entertainment* book for your honeymoon destination so you can use restaurant and other coupons, too.

❧ Avoid the high cost of a taxi; take advantage of your hotel's shuttle service or public transportation instead.

❧ If you're honeymooning abroad, play it safe by using traveler's checks or a credit card, both of which offer protection in case of loss or theft. For the best exchange rates, however, bring along your bank debit card, which usually offers better exchange rates than credit cards.

❧ Tell everyone you're on your honeymoon—you'll be surprised how many freebies this news will bring!

I have one more tip for you—it doesn't have anything to do with saving money, but with coping and saving your sanity as you plan your wedding and honeymoon. If you're like most grooms, you'll begin to feel a little helpless as you watch your dear bride and her mother rising to the top of the stress meter as they become immersed in the hundreds of decisions and arrangements that need to be made. And, unfortunately, the tighter the wedding budget, the more they'll be trying to do themselves, which adds to the anxiety. So, what can you do to help? Here are a few suggestions:

❧ Offer to help delegate some of their responsibilities.

❧ Offer to help with the calling; for example, you can telephone caterers, dance bands, photographers, etc. asking for price quotes or brochures.

❦ Help assemble the guest list, especially from your side of the family.

❦ Help your fiancée write thank-you notes. (Yes, this is one of your duties, especially when the gift comes from one of your friends or relatives!)

❦ Take your bride by the hand and "run away from home" as often as you can; she needs a break from the planning once in a while or she'll burn out.

❦ Keep your sense of humor and encourage your bride to "lighten up"; after all, your object is to become husband and wife, and as long as that's accomplished, a couple of little snafus won't really matter anyway.

By now, your notebook is full of jots and scribbles and you're more than ready for the "bottom line." This we'll finally cover in the next chapter where you'll have the opportunity to determine your own personal wedding budget. If this book has encouraged you in the way I intended, you must suspect what I already know—the next chapter will help you devise the perfect plan for you!

I wish you the best as you plan your wedding and honeymoon!

❦ ❦ ❦

13

Bottom-Line Time

(Budgets for All Price Ranges)

This is the chapter you've been waiting for! Finally, you'll be able to set up your own wedding budget. I'll help you determine how much money you'll have and how you should spend it.

I've taken all the cost-cutting plans for each category and arranged them for your consideration. You'll need to choose one "plan" from each of the thirteen categories.

Bride's Dress

Something Borrowed	$ 75
Rent It	150
Prom It	140
Bridesmaid's Gown in White	150
Distress-Sale Dress	150
Free Seamstress	190
Hire a Seamstress	415
Buy From a Resale Shop	50–75% off retail
Buy Discount	150+
The Bridal Suit	160

Bride's Headpiece and Veil

Something Borrowed	$ 0
Rent It	20
Distress Sale	20
Free Seamstress	23
Hire a Seamstress	60
Buy Discount	75

Bride's Slip

Something Borrowed	$ 0

Rent It	15–20
Free Seamstress	10
Hire a Seamstress	60
Buy Discount	40

Bride's Shoes

Something Borrowed	$ 0
Buy Discount	20
Buy Skimmers	30

Flowers

Free Florist	$ 206
Fool Them with Silks	364
Supermarket Wedding Package	400
Fool Them with the Real Thing	500
The Combination Plan	650
Share the Joy	675

Reception Food

The Family Plan	$ 219
Cake and Beverage Only	744
The Pro-Am Combo	918
Amateur Hor d'Oeuvres	1,170
Amateur Breakfast Buffet	1,332
Amateur Luncheon Buffet	1,539
Amateur Dinner Buffet	1,812
Hire the Parish Crew	3,600

Wedding Cake

Dummy Cake + Donated Sheet Cakes	$ 90
Dummy Cake + Bake-Your-Own Sheet Cakes	135
Buy a Supermarket Cake	175
Buy from a Private Party	200
Smaller Wedding Cake + Side Cakes	250

Ceremony Music

Free Recital	$ 0
Pro-Am Combo	75
Canned and Fresh	75
All Local Talent	150

Reception Music

Free Recital	$ 0
Piped-in Music	0
Amateur DJ	0
Party Tapes	0
Two-for-One Sale	100
All Local Talent	250

Decorations $ 300

Photography

Amateur Photographer	$ 93
Amateur With Rented Camera	163
Artistry Only	450
Find a Reasonable Photographer	800

Videography

Amateur Videographer	$ 15
Amateur With Rented Camera	65
Two Amateurs With Rented Cameras	130
Find a Reasonable Videographer	200

Potpourri $ 878

This is *your* menu. The choices you make from this menu are *your* choices—not your friend's or your aunt's or sister's. Only you know what is most important to you. Only you know your own emotions. When you arrive at your final budget, it will be uniquely yours. You'll need to weigh each category and select a plan that suits you. In some cases you may even decide to pay full retail price and save in other ways. In any case, don't let anyone rob you of the privilege of making your own decisions.

Beware of the well-meaning people in your life who may try to influence you, some with blatant advice, others with a more subtle approach. Your Aunt Minnie may chastise you in her own "sweet" way with, "You certainly aren't going to wear a homemade dress, are you, Dear?'' Perhaps she was a "Depression child," always wore hand-me-downs, and is enjoying your planning for vicarious reasons. She wants you to have a new wedding gown off the retail rack, regardless of cost. However, unless she plans to pay for it, don't let her remarks influence you. If ever there was a time in your life when you need to keep your head and stand on your own integrity, it is now. If you decide to have your wedding gown sewn for you, it's your decision.

One bride I spoke with recently said she couldn't care less about having a wedding gown around the house for the next forty years, so she decided to rent one. Her only goal was to look fabulous on her wedding day. She let the photographer capture the memories of her gown and she put the money she saved toward the honeymoon!

Another bride, who happens to be Assyrian, had very sentimental feelings about her wedding gown. It seems that it's traditional in her family to "embalm" the gown and then drag it out for future generations to fondle and goggle. She did want to save money, however, so she chose to have her gown sewn.

You'll need to make up your own mind about your wedding gown, as well as all your other purchases. You may feel strongly that the sanctuary should be loaded to capacity with professionally arranged flower baskets, even if it does leave meager funds for the reception. Or you may be determined to put on an award-winning feast for your guests, while filling the church with free lilacs from Grandma's backyard.

As you can see, you must make choices. What feels right to you? What means the most? You may find it helpful to take a piece of paper, draw a line down the middle, and make two lists. On the left side of the paper, write down the things that mean the most to you. On the right side of the paper, write down the things that are less important.

Sit back and look at your lists. They'll help you create your very own personalized wedding budget from the plans offered in the menu above. Just remember that to spend "more" doesn't necessarily mean "better."

To give you an idea of how this will work, I have randomly selected various plans from the menu above that resulted in the sample budgets that follow. Remember, these budgets are only *examples*. Your budget may not resemble any of them, but they'll demonstrate how easy it is to construct budgets within various price ranges.

THE "I FEEL LIKE I JUST WON THE LOTTERY!" BUDGET $2,011

Bride's Dress, "Rent It"	$ 150
Bride's Veil, "Rent It"	20
Bride's Slip, "Rent It"	20
Bride's Shoes, "Buy Discount"	20
Flowers, "Free Florist"	206
Reception Food, "The Family Plan"	219

Wedding Cake, "Dummy Cake + Donated"	90
Ceremony Music, "Free Recital"	0
Reception Music, "Free Recital"	0
Decorations	300
Photography, "Amateur Photographer"	93
Videography, "Amateur Videographer"	15
Potpourri	878
Total	$2,011

THE "NO ONE WILL EVER BELIEVE IT" BUDGET $2,867

Bride's Dress, "Bridesmaid's Dress in White"	$ 150
Bride's Veil, "Free Seamstress"	23
Bride's Slip, "Free Seamstress"	10
Bride's Shoes, "Buy Skimmers"	30
Flowers, "Fool Them With Silks"	364
Reception Food, "Cake and Beverage Only"	744
Wedding Cake, "Dummy Cake + Bake Your Own"	135
Ceremony Music, "Pro-Am Combo"	75
Reception Music, "Amateur DJ"	0
Decorations	300
Photography, "Amateur Photographer"	93
Videographer, "Amateur With Rented Camera"	65
Potpourri	878
Total	$2,867

THE "BIG SIGH OF RELIEF" BUDGET $3,150

Bride's Dress, "The Distress-Sale Dress"	$ 100
Bride's Veil, "The Distress-Sale Veil"	20
Bride's Slip, "Free Seamstress"	10
Bride's Shoes, "Buy Skimmers"	30
Flowers, "Fool Them With the Real Thing"	500
Reception Food, "Cake and Beverage Only"	744

Wedding Cake, "Buy From a Private Party"	200
Ceremony Music, "Pro-Am Combo"	75
Reception Music, "Amateur DJ"	0
Decorations	300
Photography, "Amateur With Rented Camera"	163
Videography, "Two Amateurs With Rented Cameras"	130
Potpourri	878
Total	$3,150

THE "CAN'T STOP GRINNING" BUDGET $4,091

Bride's Dress, "Hire a Seamstress"	$ 415
Bride's Veil, "Hire a Seamstress"	60
Bride's Slip, "Hire a Seamstress"	60
Bride's Shoes, "Buy Skimmers"	30
Flowers, "Fool Them With the Real Thing"	500
Reception Food, "The Pro-Am Combo"	918
Wedding Cake, "Buy a Supermarket Cake"	175
Ceremony Music, "Pro-Am Combo"	75
Reception Music, "Two-for-One Sale"	100
Decorations	300
Photography, "Artistry Only"	450
Videography, "Two Amateurs With Rented Cameras"	130
Potpourri	878
Total	$4,091

THE "GET TO KEEP THE CAR AFTER ALL" BUDGET $4,753

Bride's Dress, "Hire a Seamstress"	$ 415
Bride's Veil, "Buy Discount"	75
Bride's Slip, "Hire a Seamstress"	60
Bride's Shoes, "Buy Skimmers"	30
Flowers, "Share the Joy"	675
Reception Food, "Amateur Hors d'Oeuvres"	1,170

Wedding Cake, "Smaller Cake + Side Cakes"	250
Ceremony Music, "All Local Talent"	150
Reception Music, "Two-for-One Sale"	100
Decorations	300
Photography, "Artistry Only"	450
Videography, "Find a Reasonable Videographer"	200
Potpourri	878
Total	**$4,753**

THE "MONEY LEFT OVER FOR A HONEYMOON" BUDGET $7,988

Bride's Dress, "Hire a Seamstress"	$ 415
Bride's Veil (Buy retail)	150
Bride's Slip, "Buy Discount"	40
Bride's Shoes, "Buy Skimmers"	30
Flowers, "Share the Joy"	675
Reception Food, "Hire the Parish Crew"	3,600
Wedding Cake, "Smaller Cake + Side Cakes"	250
Ceremony Music, "All Local Talent"	150
Reception Music, "All Local Talent"	500
Decorations	300
Photography, "Find a Reasonable Photographer"	800
Videography, "Find a Reasonable Videographer"	200
Potpourri	878
Total	**$7,988**

THE "RICH AND FAMOUS EVEN LOVE IT" BUDGET $9,703

Bride's Dress (Buy retail)	$1,500
Bride's Veil (Buy retail)	150
Bride's Slip (Buy retail)	125
Bride's Shoes (Buy retail)	100
Flowers (Pay full retail price)	1,100

Reception Food, "Hire the Parish Crew"	3,600
Wedding Cake (Buy retail)	550
Ceremony Music, "All Local Talent"	150
Reception Music, "All Local Talent"	250
Decorations	300
Photography, "Find a Reasonable Photographer"	800
Videography, "Find a Reasonable Videographer"	200
Potpourri	878
Total	$9,703

As you look over these budgets and realize how much money you can save on your wedding, I'm sure you're wondering if it's really, honest-to-goodness possible to pull this off. I can tell you without reservation that it is. After hearing from so many brides in response to this book, and after serving as a consultant and seminar leader to hundreds of couples as well, I can tell you for a fact that thousands upon thousands of dollars have been saved, without jeopardizing the quality of the weddings.

Because this is exactly what I want for you—a high quality wedding on an affordable budget—I thought you might appreciate seeing excerpts of a few of the thousands of letters I've received from brides who have used the ideas in this book.

Here are four of my favorite true stories of "big weddings on small budgets." The first is a recent wedding, followed by three economical weddings that took place a few years ago and are included here because the clever ideas are still practical today, although they would probably cost about 15 percent more in today's dollars:

TEHACHAPI, CALIFORNIA   Total Cost: $5,435.36

The bride and groom paid for the entire wedding themselves, and their goal was to stay within their budget and not have to borrow money. The bride wrote me: "I can't begin to thank you enough for your book *How to Have a Big Wedding on a Small Budget* . . . we were able to have a wonderful wedding and not end up in debt."

The couple's children were part of the wedding, with the groom's son serving as a groomsman, the bride's daughter as a bridesmaid, plus her son gave her away.

Here are some interesting comments from her letter:

> ❦ She said that she put together the loose-leaf notebook I suggested and that it was her constant companion; it kept everything in one place and was "such a tremendous help."

❦ She saved money on her bridal gown by purchasing a bridesmaid's gown at a bridal shop for $200, added to the cost of her undergarments and shoes, brought the total to $311.

❦ Although they toyed with the idea of getting by with suits, the guys finally broke down and decided to rent tuxes, which totaled $333.76.

❦ Her maid-of-honor and young daughter needed compatible bridesmaids' gowns, which became a real challenge. She found a dress she liked in a catalog in a bridal salon, then found a seamstress who copied the gowns from the picture in the catalog. The maid-of-honor's gown cost $145 and her daughter's was $125.

❦ Silk flowers were used for all the flower arrangements, bouquets, boutonnieres and corsages, with the altar arrangements serving double-duty by embellishing the cake table at the reception. Tulle netting was used to drape between the pews and around the pillars, with tulle bows at the end of each pew. The silk flowers and the rest of the floral supplies were purchased in the flower district in downtown Los Angeles, which she found to be much less expensive than purchasing from a retail floral/craft supply store. Her total for all the flowers and other decorating supplies came to $515.

❦ The reception was held at the town's recreation center, for a total cost of $300, plus $40 to reserve the center for decorating the day before (4 hours @ $10 per hour).

❦ Balloons were used to make centerpieces for the tables at the reception. The balloons "grew" out of sheer frosted gift bags stuffed with green tissue. There was also a balloon arch at the entryway, behind the bride's table and the cake table. The cost of the balloons and her "balloon person" who helped create these balloon decorations was $220.

❦ She said the theme of her reception was a combination of a "balloon theme" and a "park theme." They rented white tables, chairs, picket fences and street lamps, plus she borrowed twelve white lattice panels and an arch, which were embellished with ivy, tulle netting, silk wisteria and freesia. Their local nursery let them borrow trees and shrubs to set around, plus they hauled the park bench from her own front porch, which came in handy for photo opps. The rental costs totaled $670.63.

❧ Amazingly, a caterer was able to provide a luncheon buffet for only $3.43 per person, which came to a total of about $800.

❧ The wedding cake was baked by a local person for $1.65 per slice. They only ordered enough cake to feed half the guests, since so many wedding guests don't eat dessert, which turned out to be a wise decision since they still had cake left over! She made her own cake top from silk flowers, so the total cost for the cake came to only $165.

❧ Music turned out to be a negligible expense because the church organist played for the ceremony at a cost of only $50 and friends provided the music for the reception at a cost of $250. The reception musicians played Celtic music on mandolin, violin and guitar, which "was relaxing and a nice change—everyone enjoyed them."

❧ By purchasing the proof book, instead of an album, and because a friend provided the reception photos as a wedding gift, the total cost of the photography was only $500.

❧ Thanks to a friend who is a professional printer, they were able to purchase invitations and thank-you notes at his cost. He also printed map cards for the out-of-town guests. The total, including postage, came to $228.73.

Some of their incidental costs included:

Guest book*	$ 38.53
Pen for guest book	17.00
Wedding hostess	30.00
Church sound technician	30.00
Unity candle & holder**	53.54
Garters	16.00
Favors (pastel colored M&M's w/tulle & ribbon)	20.00
Total	$205.07

*(Also served as an album and memory book)
**(The unity candle holds the wedding invitation and, along with the crystal stand, are keepsakes.)

The bride sent me eight wedding photos, which gave visual proof that you *can* have a lovely, elegant wedding for less than $5,500. I wish you could see her photos—you would be inspired and encouraged as you plan your own wedding on a small budget.

The bride received a copy of this book from her fiancé at the same time she received her engagement ring. She wrote that the book "allowed us to have a 'classy' wedding at an inexpensive price."

Here are some of the ways that did it:

❧ Bridesmaids' bouquets homemade of white silk flowers, embellished with ivy, string pearls by-the-yard and a hot-glue gun.

❧ Homemade ring bearer's pillow.

❧ Boutonnieres made by the bride and her mother several months before the wedding from packaged silk flowers, imitation rose leaves and a little baby's breath.

❧ Candles purchased from a wholesale candle outlet that were "cheaper by the dozen."

❧ Ceremony site decorated with fresh greenery stripped from cedar trees in the North Carolina mountains (several garbage bags full) and "tied together" with floral wire.

❧ Bride's veil made by her mother at a cost of $13, a copy of one they had seen in a salon for about $150.

❧ Bride's gown purchased at 50 percent off retail at an outlet store in Reading, Ohio.

❧ Used a professional florist only for the center table arrangement at the reception, the bride's going-away corsage and one large arrangement for the front of the church. Total cost: $85.

❧ Bride's father made the kneeling bench, which was donated to the church after the wedding.

❧ They used the existing Christmas "plug-in" candles, plus added greenery and a white bow to all eight windows. Bows were also added to the first three pews.

❧ The bride and her fiancé decorated the reception site the day before the wedding (pinned netting, ribbons, bows and great swags of tulle across the fronts of all the tables).

- The reception food was made by the bride, the bride's mother and a friend of the family. Another friend served as a supervisor to help keep the trays filled during the reception.

- Professional cake; paid $180. It had two sections joined by a stairway. One section had four layers and the other three, plus they added one large Styrofoam layer to give the cake a higher, more dramatic look.

- Used a professional photographer.

The bride wrote, "David and I cannot thank you enough for your input in our wedding. The entire sha-bang was only $3,000 . . . my sister spent more than that on her reception alone." Because they saved so much on their wedding, they were able to splurge on their honeymoon—a Western Caribbean cruise.

By the way, their only wedding glitch involved the photographer's equipment and the bridesmaids' street clothes which had been locked into a dressing room, for which there was *no* key! The bride wrote, "The custodian had no key; the preacher had no key; the church secretary had no key. My brother-in-law opened the door with a credit card, and I thought that was only in the movies!"

BALTIMORE, MARYLAND   Total Cost: $3,731

Believe it or not, this couple's wedding and honeymoon *combined* totaled $3,731, and here are some of the clever things they did to pull this off:

- Purchased the bride's gown off a sale rack at a bridal salon for $282. (She saw the identical gown at another shop for $750 retail.)

- Alterations done for free by the groom's mother who also made the bride's petticoat for $17 and a "gorgeous" headpiece and veil for $25.

- Bride wore her own white flat shoes and jewelry.

- Purchased bridesmaids' dresses from a JCPenney outlet store for under $50 each. (She wrote that some were as low as $30.)

- Wedding cake baked by a woman who bakes cakes at her home; charged $.84 per slice. (The usual retail bakery in her area charges from $1 to $3 per slice.)

- They found a restaurant with a "gorgeous, waterfront location," where brunch was served at $8 per person, which included free use of a room for the ceremony itself, plus use of an outside deck. The bride wrote,

"The location had a spectacular view with the early morning sunlight dancing on the water and the boats all around the marina . . . I'm sure our guests must have thought we spent a fortune." By the way, the $8 figure is $4 off the restaurant's regular brunch menu price because the bride "negotiated away" some of the fancier items, such as the Eggs Benedict topped with crab, which left them scrambled eggs, bacon, sausage, home fries, muffins, bagels with cream cheese, pancakes, French toast, a beautiful fruit display, coffee, tea and orange juice. (The bride said that in the Baltimore/Washington, DC metro area you would usually pay as little as $10 to as much as $130 per person, with $40 being the average.)

❧ The bride purchased blank invitations (in packages of 50 for $6) at a stationery outlet, and a friend had them printed as a gift.

❧ All the flowers were free—a gift from a member of their family who happens to be a professional florist. (At first, he was going to sell them the flowers at his wholesale cost of $100, but just days before the wedding he told the bride that the flowers would be his gift to them.)

❧ Photography and videography—all done by friends and family members who were amateurs.

❧ Played taped music for the reception.

The bride wrote, "I never felt more special or beautiful than I did on my wedding day, and when my husband saw me coming down the aisle, he got misty and looked at me like he never had before. When it comes right down to it, *that* is what weddings are all about—not how much you spend! We saved so much money that we could afford a week-long honeymoon on the sunny beaches of Florida. By going off-season we saved tons of money there as well. We spent a Grand Total of $3,731 on the entire wedding and honeymoon *combined*! I'm sure everyone thought we spent thousands more. With a little creativity and ingenuity, other couples will be able to do it, too. I know it sounds hopelessly cliche, but if we can do it, just about anyone can!"

BUTTE, MONTANA   Total Cost: $3,388

Although this couple lives in Seattle, they had to plan a long-distance wedding because both their families live in Montana. The bride wrote, "This was a challenge at times, but having a wedding there (in Butte) instead of Seattle saved us quite a lot."

There were 250 guests at the wedding, and this is exactly what the couple spent:

Bride's gown, sewn by a Seattle seamstress	$ 400
Bride's makeup and hair, done by a friend	0

Rented hoop petticoat	8
Veil, made by the bride	15
Shoes & hosiery, discount	30
Rented bridesmaids' dresses (split the cost)	50
Bridesmaids' & groomsmen's gifts (6 @ $20)	120
Reception hall rental	250
Photographer (a retired man with experience)	265
Cake (baked by a private party)	150
Video (by bride's brother)	0
Caterer (a family friend who runs a catering business out of her home, @ $2.50 per person)	675
DJ (for reception)	225
Minister's fee (bride's father)	0
Organist & soloist (friends of the family who performed for free, but bride bought gifts)	30
Trumpeters (2)	120
Flowers (the bride made them up in silks ahead of time—shopped discount)	200
Decorations, balloons & misc.	100
Groom's tuxedo, plus split cost of groomsmens'	150
Potpourri	600

The bride wrote that the only problem on her wedding day was that the hoop skirt didn't work well under her wedding gown (she had neglected to try it on ahead of time!) which resulted in a full hour's worth of emergency "fixins" right before the service began. Other than that, everything went off without a hitch and, if the photographs are any indication, the wedding had an elegant, expensive look and the bride was beautiful, cranky hoop skirt, or not!

Finally, I thought you might enjoy seeing a breakdown of the costs for our daughter's wedding, which totaled $3,530:

Bridal Attire		
	Wedding dress	$ 400
	Veil	120
	Slip	50
	Shoes	24
Florist		289
Reception Food		990

Wedding Cake	185
Music	
One vocalist	25
Four musicians @ $40 per musician	160
Decorations	110
Nursery Care	45
Photography	500
Videography (Gift)	0
Potpourri	
Ice sculpture	50
225 Invitations	85
300 Napkins	35
Thank-you notes	24
Postage	60
Church custodian	50
Church sound man	25
Church coordinator	35
Favors	20
Slide developing (for reception slide show)	15
Dry-cleaning bills (last-minute pressing)	24
Last-minute alterations	25
Throw-away garter	5
Supermarket flowers (for cake and buffet table)	18
Bride's blood test and exam	40
Guest book	6
Ring bearer's pillow	7
Special calligraphy pen	10
Mints	10
Hair appointments	36
Sheet music/organist	6
Bridesmaids' headpieces	6
Paper plates/forks for cake	28
Baskets for distributing favors	12
Total	$3,530

As you will recall from the Introduction, we faced these expenses at a time when we were not prepared; we definitely did not have a "wedding fund" as we should have. However, because our daughter paid for all her own wedding clothes, and the groom's parents generously helped toward the reception food, we were able to squeeze the money out of our budget over a four-month period. This meant that our law-student son needed to borrow a little more than he had planned on that year's student loan, but he was more than happy to do this. So it all worked out, paying cash as we went.

How are you going to handle your wedding expenses? You can juggle things around as we did, or I have some other suggestions:

- ❧ Do you have any savings bonds you can sell?

- ❧ Do you have any other available savings you can use?

- ❧ Do you have an extra vehicle you can sell?

- ❧ How about the small lot you inherited from Uncle Octavio several years ago? Could it be sold quickly?

- ❧ Do you have an insurance policy with cash value?

- ❧ How about the stamp, baseball card or coin collection?

- ❧ Why not have a huge family garage sale? Ask the relatives if they would donate their castaways to the cause. People will buy anything!

- ❧ What about borrowing money? This is a very serious question because you don't want the emotion of the moment to leave you with a debt that will become a serious burden to your family after the wedding. Be very careful!

❧

Remember the first section of your notebook called "The Budget"? This is where you'll need to enter the exact budget plan you have selected, as well as the source of monies you'll have available. You should also enter the dollar amount for each category at the top of the other sections in your notebook. Keep these figures close to your heart as you're out and about making your purchases; then enter your actual purchases in your notebook daily so that you'll know where you stand all the time.

One word of caution to the mother of the bride: Don't get caught in the trap of trying to give your daughter a wedding that's what you really wanted when you were married, but didn't have. It's so easy to get caught up in vicarious planning—living out the romance and excitement through your daughter. Believe me, if you stay on the budget you select, she'll be just as happy a year from now than if you had lost your head and gone out of control, and you won't have all those bills to pay!

This is a time for mature restraint, but it can still be one of the most rewarding and creative things you have ever done! You'll see!

14

I Think I Can,
I Think I Can...

(Putting It All Together)

Have you ever watched a group of women as they make a personalized quilt? They lovingly and painstakingly create individual squares that are finally sewn together. In the beginning stages the quilt doesn't look like much, but the individual squares form a true work of art as they are fitted together. During this process a peculiar thing happens—the underside becomes quite a mess. There are wads of strings and knots and, seemingly, no pattern at all. And yet, if it weren't for these ugly, messy pieces of thread and yarn, there could never be the pretty design on top.

Your wedding plans will seem at times like a quilt. One of the squares will have a flower on it; you'll work patiently on this square until it finally looks good enough to add to the rest of your handiwork. Your food square will be full of tiny details and it will also take patience, but when it's complete, it, too, will be ready to join your other lovely squares.

As you're working along, the underside of your quilt will become a mass of strings and knots. Your floral square might have a dangling strand of ribbon, exchanged three times before its color seems exactly right; your food square may have a big knot caused by your frustration and indecision. From time to time, your life in general may even seem like strings and knots, for occasionally your mind will feel cluttered and often your den will be, too. You'll have price lists sitting on top of catalogs, and pictures of wedding cakes intermingled with the fabric you purchased to make the covered umbrellas. But when things seem confusing, just say to yourself, "I'm only looking at the underside of the quilt!" However, the time will come, and sooner than you think, when you'll be able to stand back and see the finished product. What a thrill that will be for you!

Meanwhile, diligently use your notebook. Accept and enjoy your role as wedding coordinator. Consider it a great privilege and opportunity to be able to use your abilities in this way. And remember that all your expertise won't go to waste, for perhaps you'll have another wedding to plan some day, or you may even have a dear friend who needs your help. The knowledge and experience you'll gain through this planning can be wonderfully useful in the future.

Just consider yourself a master quilter as you make those phone calls, talk to those florists and tie up the pew bows. All the pieces will come together in the end and it'll be worth all the work.

I've been through this entire creative process, so I have empathy for you. I've stood at the beginning, where you're standing now, with all of your questions and frustrations. But, I made it through to the end where I was able to stand back and admire my beautiful quilt!

Your quilt will be a beauty and it will probably win a prize. I can see it now:

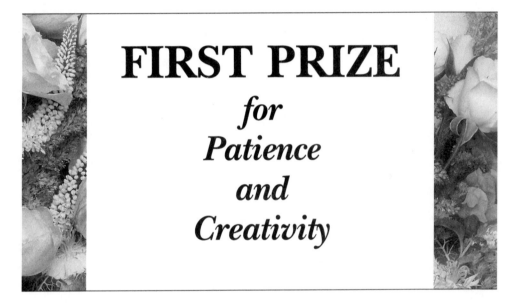

FIRST PRIZE
for
Patience
and
Creativity

Remember the positive attitude we talked about in the first chapter? Now is the time to kick it into gear! Put that smile on your face and remember that I'm cheering for you!

You can do it!

Resources

Bridal Consultants

Association of Bridal Consultants
(860) 355-0464
www.bridalassn.com
June Wedding, Inc.
(702) 474-9558
www.junewedding.com
Weddings Beautiful Worldwide
(804) 288-1220
www.weddingsbeautiful.com

Bridal Registries

Bed Bath & Beyond
(800) GO BEYOND
www.bedbathandbeyond.com
Bloomingdales
(800) 888-2WED
www.bloomingdales.com
Dillard's
(800) 626-6001
www.dillards.com
The Home Depot
www.homedepot.com
Linen 'N Things
(800) 568-8765
www.lnt.com
Macy's Wedding Channel
(888) 92-BRIDES
www.macys.weddingchannel.com
Neiman Marcus
www.neimanmarcus.com
Pier I Imports
(800) 245-4595
www.pier1.com
Target's Gift Registry Club Wedd
(800) 888-9333
www.target.com
The Wedding List
(800) 345-7795
www.theweddinglist.com

Wedding Gowns $800 and Under

ABS by Allen Schwartz
(212) 398-0330
www.absstyle.com

Alfred Angelo
(800) 528-3589
www.alfredangelo.com
America's Bridal Discounters
(800) 326-0833
www.bridaldiscounters.com
Amsale
(800) 765-0170
www.amsale.com
An Alternative
(Kansas City gown rentals)
(888) 761-8686
BestPromDresses.com
(888) 217-5655
www.bestpromdresses.com
Bonny Gowns
(800) 528-0030
www.bonny.com
Bridal Marketplace
(800) 968-0338
www.bridalmarketplace.com
Bridal Originals
(800) 876-4696
www.bridaloriginals.com
Bridal Warehouse, Inc.
www.usabridal.com
BrideSave.com
(888) 321-GOWN
www.bridesave.com
David's Bridal
(800) 399-2743
www.davidsbridal.com
Discount Bridal Service
(800) 874-8794
www.discountbridalservice.com
Discount Gloves
(800) 479-4696
www.bridalgloves.com
Ebay
www.ebay.com
Eden Bridals, Inc.
(800) 828-8831
www.edenbridals.com
Filene's Basement (Boston)
(617) 542-2011

Forever Yours International
(800) USA-Bride
www.foreverbridals.com
Formals, Etc.
(800) 943-6762
www.formalsetc.com
GownsOnline.com
(800) 776-4696
www.gownsonline.com
Jacquelin Bridals
(239) 277-7099
www.jacquelinbridals.com
Jasmine
(800) 634-0224
www.jasminebridal.com
JCPenney outlet stores
(800) 222-6161
www.jcpenney.com
Jessica McClintock
(800) 333-5301
www.jessicamcclintock.com
Jessica McClintock outlet stores
San Francisco
(415) 553-8390
Mont Clair, CA
(909) 982-1866
Huntington Beach, CA
(714) 841-7124
El Paso, TX
(915) 771-9550
The Knot
www.theknot.com
Maggie Sottero Couture Bridal
(801) 255-3870
www.maggiesotterobridal.com
Mary's Bridal
(281) 933-9678
www.marysbridal.com
Mon Chéri Bridals, Inc.
(609) 530-1900
www.mcbridals.com
Monique Bridal
(626) 401-9910
www.moniquebridal.com
Moonlight Design, Inc.
(800) 447-0405
www.moonlightbridal.com
Mori Lee, Inc.
www.morileeinc.com

Price Less Bridals
(818) 340-6514
www.bargainweddinggown.com
Priscilla of Boston
(617) 242-2677
Private Label by G
(800) 858-3338
www.privatelabelbyg.com
RK Bridal
(800) 929-9512
www.rkbridal.com
Sweetheart Gowns
(800) 324-3242
www.gowns.com

Affordable Wedding Attire for the Wedding Party

(See also "Wedding Gowns $800 and Under." Some of these sources may carry wedding party attire as well.)

A La Mode
www.veilsalamode.com
Affordable headpieces and accessories
www.romanticheadlines.com
Affordable wedding veils
www.whitehotweddings.com
An Alternative (rentals in Kansas City)
(888) 761-8686
Autumn Moon Designs
www.bridalstuff.com
BestBridesmaid.com
www.bestbridesmaid.com
BestPromDresses
www.bestpromdresses.com
Bill Levkoff
(800) LEVKOFF
Chadwick's of Boston
(800) 525-6650
www.chadwicks.com
Discount Dyeables
www.discountdyeables.com
ETuxedo.com
www.etuxedo.com
Formals, Etc. (rentals)
www.formalsetc.com
4Tuxedos.com
www.4tuxedos.com
MarryingMan.com
www.marryingman.com

Melissa Sweet Bridal Collection
(404) 633-4395
www.melissasweet.com
Romantic Headlines
www.romanticheadlines.com
Tux Town and Classic Collection
(tux rentals by mail)
(800) 824-0047

Wedding Business Consumer Action
Better Business Bureau's OnLine
Reliability Web Site (check out a
company's reputation)
www.bbbonline.org
Call your local Better Business Bureau
BEFORE signing up!

Wedding Entertainment
American Disc Jockey Association
(301) 705-5150
www.adja.org
American Federation of Musicians
(800) NLA-7007
The Ultimate Wedding Song Library
www.ultimatewedding.com/songs/

Wedding Invitations
American Wedding Album
(800) 428-0379
www.theamericanwedding.com
Ashton Wedding Invitations, Inc.
www.ourbeginning.com
Catalog Orders Headquarters
www.catalog.orders.com
Discount Invitations
(888) 969-9394
www.discount-invitations.com
Invitation & Promotion Hotline
(800) 800-4355
www.invitationhotline.com
Invitations By Dawn
(800) 332-3296
www.invitationsbydawn.com
Invitesite
www.invitesite.com
PaperDirect
(800) 272-7377
www.paperdirect.com

Paper Style
(888) 670-5300
www.paperstyle.com
Reaves Engraving
(910) 610-4499
www.reavesengraving.com
Regency
(800) 423-4396
www.regencythermo.com
Rexcraft
(800) 635-3898
www.rexcraft.com
WeddingBells
www.weddingbells.com
WedNet
www.wednet.com

Wedding Photography
Photoworks.com
www.photoworks.com
PrimeShot.com
(888) 708-9593
www.primeshot.com
Professional Photographers
of America, Inc.
www.ppa.com
Waterhouse Books
(860) 526-1296
www.waterhousebooks.com

Wedding Supplies
American Rental Association
(800) 334-2177
www.ararental.org
BJ's Wholesale Club, Inc.
www.bjswholesale.com
Butterfly Celebration
(800) 548-3284
www.butterflycelebration.com
Chandler's Candle Company Inc.
(800) 463-7143
www.chandlerscandle.com
C.O.D. Wholesale
(888) 345-0418
www.codwholesale.com
Costco
www.costco.com
EZ Bow Maker
(800) 311-6529

FlowerSales.com
  (800) 950-SEND
  www.flowersales.com
Hobby Lobby (supplies & rentals)
  (405) 745-1100
  www.hobbylobby.com
Michaels (arts & crafts)
  (800) 642-4235
  www.michaels.com
MJDesigns
  (972) 621-8585
  www.mjdesigns.com
Oriental Trading Company
  www.orientaltrading.com
Sam's Club
  www.samsclub.com
Tender Seed Company
  (509) 962-6631
  www.tenderseedcompany.com
Tree & Floral Beginnings
  (800) 499-9580
  www.plantamemory.com
2GRoses
  (800) 880-0735
  www.freshroses.com
UniqueFavors.com
  (800) 756-6184
  www.uniquefavors.com

Wedding Venues
USA CityLink
  www.usacitylink.com

Wedding Links Galore
  www.weddinglinksgalore.com
WeddingChannel.com
  www.weddingchannel.com

Wedding Videography
Wedding and Event Videographers
Association International (WEVA)
  (800) 501-WEVA
  www.weva.com

Wedding Web Sites
www.bridalmarketplace.com
www.brideagain.com
www.brides.com
www.bridesave.com
www.dreamweavers.com
www.frugalbride.com
www.ibride.com
www.ourbeginning.com
www.theknot.com
www.todaysbride.com
www.ultimatewedding.com
www.weddingbells.com
www.weddingcentral.com
www.weddingchannel.com
www.weddingdetails.com
www.weddinghelpers.com
www.weddingspot.com
www.whitehotweddings.com

Index

To the Reader

I'm constantly updating this book and could use your help. Please write me to let me know how this book worked for you, and send me your own unique cost-cutting tips, plus any price variations you find in your region of the country. Also, I have a big bulletin board in my office for my readers' wedding photos. Do you have an extra for me?

Thanks so much,

Diane Warner
c/o Betterway Books
4700 East Galbraith Road
Cincinnati, Ohio 45236

By the way, you're welcome to drop by and visit my Web site anytime. I'd love to "see" you!

www.dianewarnerbooks.com

Personalize Your Wedding With Elegant Handmade Accessories and Decorations!

Beautiful Bridal Accessories You Can Make—Here's a smart, sophisticated alternative to store-bought wedding accessories. Jacquelynne Johnson shows you how to make an incredible variety of elegant adornments for the bride and wedding party, and how to make cherished keepsakes to commemorate your special day. Personalized to fit your style, each of these 22 step-by-step projects is inexpensive and easy-to-make with simple embellishing techniques and a glue gun. And while the vast majority of the projects are "no-sew," those projects requiring a little needle and thread can be mastered by beginners in minutes.
ISBN 1-55870-624-0 ✳ paperback ✳ 128 pages ✳ #70570-K

Creative Wedding Florals You Can Make—Create your very own floral arrangements for priceless wedding memories with a personal touch. Terry Rye will teach you step-by-step how to design more than 20 stunning designs. You'll find something for every part of the wedding—from the bride's bouquet and boutonnieres to pew decorations, table centerpieces and wedding cake toppers.
ISBN 1-55870-560-0 ✳ paperback ✳ 128 pages ✳ #70488-K

Creative Wedding Keepsakes You Can Make—Make your wedding elegant and unforgettable with these beautiful keepsake ideas. From the bridal veil to the guest book, this book provides 21 step-by-step projects that are fun, affordable and surprisingly easy to make. Best of all, each project is made from non-perishable materials, so everything can be finished well in advance of the big day.
ISBN 1-55870-559-7 ✳ paperback ✳ 128 pages ✳ #70487-K

Memory Makers® Wedding Idea Book—This unique guide combines dazzling layout ideas with easy-to-follow instructions for creating a gorgeous wedding scrapbook album. You'll find layouts for every event, including the engagement, shower, wedding ceremony, reception, honeymoon and more. Every aspect of the scrapbooking process is covered, from organizing photos and selecting an album to choosing a visual theme and writing journal entries.
ISBN 1-89212-708-3 ✳ paperback ✳ 128 pages ✳ #31788-K

These titles are available from your local art & craft retailer, bookseller, online supplier or by calling 1-800-448-0915.